02/09   2.00

Sharing the Final Journey
Walking with the Dying

Sharing the Final Journey

Walking with the Dying

Norma Wylie, R.N., M.S.N.,
Terrill A. Mast, Ph.D.
and Jay Kennerly

Published by
ROBERT POPE FOUNDATION

Distributed by
LANCELOT PRESS
Box 425, Hantsport, N.S. B0P 1P0

ISBN 0-88999-608-3
Published 1996
Cover design: Peggy Issenman

Distributed by
LANCELOT PRESS LIMITED
Hantsport, Nova Scotia.
Office and production facilities situated on Highway No. 1,
1/2 mile east of Hantsport.

MAILING ADDRESS:
P.O. Box 425, Hantsport, Nova Scotia B0P 1P0
Telephone (902) 684-9129   Fax (902) 684-3685

CONTENTS

Foreword by Dr. Jock Murray • 7

Foreword by Dr. Glen W. Davidson • 12

Introduction • 18

NORMA'S STORY — PART I • 21
The Gift of Tears

RANDY'S STORY • 39
"Time to go, Norma"

JACK'S STORY • 55
"I've been waiting for you, dear"

GEORGE'S STORY • 73
A Love Story

NAN'S STORY • 85
"Nearly me"

GARY'S STORY • 103
"Dad has something he wants to tell you, kids"

ESTHER'S STORY • 119
Ready to Die

ANN'S STORY • 131
Alzheimer's — The Long Good-Bye

NORMA'S STORY — PART II • 145
Growth through Loss

Afterword • 168
References • 176

FOREWORD

by Dr. Jock Murray

To professional skill [the physician] will join human warmth and understanding. By so doing, and only by so doing, will he accept the whole burden and fulfill his destiny. If anyone seeks happiness, here it may prove to be. It is the second mile enjoined in the text, "And whosoever shall compel thee to go a mile, go with him twain." The good physician will accompany his patient on the second mile and to the end of the road.

Sir John Parkinson
The Patient and the Physician, 1951

Pat's death was a joyous experience. Of course, it was tragic that my 50-year-old sister-in-law, who relished life, laughter, and her family, would develop a particularly malignant and unresponsive form of leukemia just as her two children were planning their marriages, and she was longing for grandchildren. She loved children, and was already a surrogate grandmother for other little ones. It seems difficult to remember her without seeing her with her head back in a great laugh, a child nestled in her arms. The large circle of family and friends initially had great difficulty dealing with the news of her illness, and the meaning of it all, but from the beginning she taught us how. When she died four months later we all recognized that we had grown in the experience, and that she had taught us how to die and how to live. We recognized that we had received a great gift. The gift was the privilege of walking with her in that last journey.

This was a singular episode in my personal life, but

Norma Wylie has walked this road many times. She has learned from this experience and in this book shares those lessons with us, through the lives of patients — each of them unique, and each with their own journey.

I was not proud of my profession in Pat's case, but I was gratified and impressed by the nurses who truly walked with Pat and her family, and who were there at every point in that journey, including the funeral. It was clear that they knew the lessons, but Pat taught them as well. Sadly, the doctors did not put themselves in a position to be taught. Brief formal ward rounds by consultants who rotate each month, stand some distance from the end of the bed to discuss blood counts and chemotherapy, prevented the physicians from learning from Pat.

Are we expecting too much of physicians who must struggle to bring the strongest, evidenced-based medical science to overcome illness? While we instruct our medical students to be experts in their diagnostic skills, we spend too little time showing them that they can also be successful in relieving suffering and providing hope, even when cure is not possible. Even when death is inevitable, there can be hope in marking a life by a dignified, successful and peaceful death.

As physicians we are by nature competitive, afraid of any lack of control, afraid of death, and instructed to flail at disease. By this process we regard death as a failure of our skill, our art, and ultimately of ourselves. To stave off this threat to our skill and our persons, we may offer false hopes, false goals, false possibilities, or worse, we walk away, unable to accept or tolerate the loss of control and the loss of the fight. We see the possibility of death as a fight for life rather than a part of life, the death of a person. It is sad, it is sometimes tragic, it sometimes comes too soon — but it comes to us all. When it comes, we wish to have it the best death it can be for us, and we wish for companions to walk that last journey along with us.

How can we convey such lessons to health professionals, so they can be better caregivers for the chronically ill and the dying? We want our students to understand the human condition, and to develop attitudes and feelings that will make them better caregivers and healers. Our traditional teaching method, striding to the front of a classroom and calling for the first slide, is clearly doomed to fail. If I thought it would come to fruition, I would suggest that every aspiring health professional accompany one person on that walk, being with them for the course of their final illness, holding their hand late at night, drinking bad coffee in the lounge with family and friends as they struggle with what to do next, being there at the moment of death, and eventually attending the funeral service, meeting those people who knew the person in an earlier healthy life through their school, job, neighborhood and evenings out. Another powerful way is through stories; stories of people, with lives and friends, and dreams and fears. That is the focus of this book, and from these stories we learn of life as well as death.

Our attitude towards death seems to have come full circle. In simpler times death was more natural, an expected and accepted part of life, and people in the community seemed to know how to respond. In more recent times death became institutionalized, regimented, more commercial, more isolated and more unspoken. A reaction to this latter change is causing us again to speak of death more openly. The discussions of advance directives and living wills, of death with dignity, euthanasia, and physician-assisted suicide, have caused us to rethink our social, cultural and medical views of the end of life. In Canada we have had the development of a new specialty of palliative medicine, but that is not adequate to address fully the needs of each of us who will die. Each of us will die, and each of us wants a dignified and comforted death that recognizes who we are, who we have been and what we have meant.

The three walkers in this volume are storytellers. Story-telling has an ageless history. In recent times it has taken on a more serious and academic aspect, with illness narrative studies as a serious literary dimension. Illness narratives are attracting increasing attention because of their understanding of the human condition, their dramatic setting for insights, and their ability to tell us about the nature of the human struggle, and ultimately of ourselves. In the criticism that sometimes arises between the conflict of the clinical case history and the patient narrative, there is a lack of recognition that there are two distinct narratives going on simultaneously. That is why I neglect all but the most cursory clinical information when discussing a patient narrative with students. As soon as I mention some clinical information, the students switch gears and begin to request detailed information on the clinical aspects, reconstructing the story on a physiological or pathological basis rather than a personal odyssey. To name the illness distracts from the person.

I am enthralled by the Navaho image of the storyteller, a round mother figure sitting with tiny children clutching all over her lap and limbs, her mouth open, her eyes to the sky, telling stories based on the wisdom of the ages. We are currently in an arrogant age that suggests that knowledge is continually outdated, and I confess to having been in that band who criticized medical literature for being out of date before seeing print, not recognizing that there is an aspect of our understanding that is forever present and calls upon each of us to continually renew. One of the ways to understand is to continually ask fundamental questions, which we each must do, and sometimes do best through storytelling.

If we wish to know a man, we ask, "What is his story, his real, inmost story?" For each of us is a biography, a story. Each of us is a singular narrative, which is constructed continually and unconsciously by, through, and in us — through our perceptions, our feelings, our thoughts, our actions; and, not least, through our discourse, our spoken narratives. Biologically, physiologically, we are not so different from each other; historically, as narratives, we are each of us unique.

Oliver Sacks, 1985

Dr. Jock Murray, OC, MD, FRCPC, FACP is Professor of Medical Humanities at Dalhousie University and Director of the Dalhousie Multiple Sclerosis Research Unit. He was Dean of Medicine at Dalhousie from 1985-1992. He has served on the Boards of many medical and community organizations. He was the founder and first President of the Dalhousie Society for the History of Medicine, Vice President of the American Academy of Neurology and President of the Canadian Neurology Society. As a lecturer and writer, Dr. Murray has given over 200 presentations on multiple sclerosis, other neurological disorders, medical education and medical history. He has recently written a small book on the illness and healing aspects of Robert Pope's art, entitled Reflections.

FOREWORD

by Dr. Glen W. Davidson

Storytelling is a reciprocal act. In a clinical setting it is, for the teller, an act of reorientation after basic change in his life. For the listener, the storytelling, which provides a window on the teller's soul, is often received as a most intimate and precious gift.

Orientation, a technical term in the mental health field, is part of the mental status examination. The term refers to a person's understanding of who he is and how he relates to others. Physicians, nurses and some other caregivers are taught how to make a mental status examination of each patient. To be oriented is to be related. The baby's search of the parent's face, the scrutiny of a spouse's countenance after long absence, the close examination of the stranger given by the elderly person with failing eyesight are all examples of the initial, almost instantaneous act we perform to determine whether we can relate to another. Change, particularly unexpected or unwanted change, alters relationships, sometimes irreversibly.

People who are ill or in shock may not be sure of the time of day, or the day of the week. Some may not know where they are. Others become so disoriented that they believe themselves to be someone else, to be living in the past or the future, and, perhaps, in another world.

Some research suggests that the average person becomes briefly disoriented many times a day but that orientation is usually recovered very quickly, even in a millisecond. However, individuals reacting to medication or other drugs, calamity, and some illnesses such as those producing high fevers or brain chemistry imbalance, may be disoriented for longer periods of time.

Whenever we encounter change we are disoriented. We have a number of skills we may use to try to help us become reoriented; such behaviors as fighting the change as though we could prevent it, fleeing the change as though we could escape, or denying the change as though we could reverse what has happened. The most effective skill, however, is asking questions, comparing experiences, contrasting what we perceive with the experience of others, even crying. This is all part of "telling the story".

People have an amazing ability to adapt — provided they are given sufficient time and the opportunity to come to grips with their situation. Telling the story of one's disorientation requires relating to another person. Whether our storytelling is with a close friend or member of our family, or a trained professional, the process is a basic and necessary part of adapting to new circumstances.

A person who is disoriented needs help. Therefore, one of the first responsibilities of members of the helping professions is to assist in the patient's reorientation. Norma Wylie provides a model for every professional, friend or family member of how to be effective in the reciprocal exchange we call human relationship.

Perhaps the biggest change in health care since the 1960s, certainly for the bereaved, is the organization of mutual help groups for every dysfunction or malady listed by the World Health Organization. What is provided by such groups, often not provided by members of the helping professions and perhaps not even offered in the family, is the modeled behavior of telling stories of loss by those who have already experienced disorientation. The stories in *Sharing the Final Journey* may be similar to some of your stories or they may be outside your experience, but either way, they represent the exchange between teller and listener which are models for us all to copy or adapt to our own needs.

Sociologist Arthur Frank, a professor at the University of Calgary, writes of people as "wounded storytellers." Sooner or later we all will be wounded storytellers. He notes that too often we think of an ill person as a "victim" of disease and the "recipient" of care. Given the chance, persons who have been afflicted and made vulnerable will transform their illnesses from fate into experience. Rather than disease setting their bodies apart from others, in the story, "the common bond of suffering ... joins bodies in their shared vulnerability...". The paradox of wounded storytellers is that their sharing of the story often becomes a gift of caring for others, rather than a plea for receiving care. "But telling does not come easy, and neither does listening. Seriously ill people are wounded not just in body but in voice. They need to become storytellers in order to recover the voices that illness and its treatment often take away."

Storytelling, then, is also story-listening — one of the least expensive and most effective acts a practitioner/therapist can perform. Too often, those of us in the helping professions — clergy, physicians, nurses, teachers — treat the patient's telling of his story as a waste of the listener's time. This assumption is wrong.

We may not think of a person's story as important for others. Most of us as children heard a grandparent telling a story of the past over and over again. To the untrained ear, the story sounded like repetition. To the trained ear, however, the story is seldom the same. The beginning or the ending may be slightly different. Whichever part of the story is altered from the previous telling suggests that the teller still is puzzled by such questions as "What happened?" "Why did it affect me?" "In what way have I been altered?" "Will I be able to accommodate, even survive, this change?"

To the untrained ear, the story may seem inaccurate, fanciful, even deceitful. To the trained ear, however, the story provides a framework within which the teller may be helped to a better understanding of himself and to reorientation with the present time and place.

Psychiatrist Robert Butler, the first director of the National Institute on Aging, was the first clinician to relate storytelling to rites of passage — the ritual process by which we make major transitions in life. Holy days and holidays are times set aside for retelling the stories which inform a people, as well as individuals, who we are and what we are about. The interviews, the holy moments of exchange between teller and listener, are important not only as an opportunity to listen for vulnerability, but also as a diagnostic tool. Butler suggested that any time a person begins to tell a reflective story, the listener should take it as a signal that the storyteller may have been disoriented by change in his life or circumstances.

Dr. Butler suggests we should begin with the premise that all patients are somewhat disoriented and encourage them to tell the stories of loss which are important to them. Rather than discouraging an elderly patient from telling a story of long ago, for example, the effective clinician will help the storyteller to be as articulate and as accurate as possible. The story, as told, puts things into context. It describes the setting in which the teller felt oriented and indicates what happened later to disorient him. The teller identifies what he values. This may be significantly different from what the listener may have thought would be of value. Too often, listeners, particularly in the helping professions, have already assumed that they know the patient's problems and try to answer unasked questions. That is very frustrating to the patient and further confuses him as he may be struggling with quite different problems.

Storytelling has returned to the health arena because of extensive research into what is normal in human growth and development. According to the work of Jean Piaget and other constructionists, each individual has specific tasks to accomplish throughout his life span. Questions relating to a younger age must be answered before questions of an older age can be defined and answered adequately. If, for example, an infant has not been able to establish a trusting relationship with another, later in life that person will have increasing difficulties in trusting not only in others but also in himself. What people tell in their stories about themselves and the way they tell their stories reveals the success they have had in handling the tasks of each stage of their development. In each telling of the stories of loss, the storyteller's task is to play out for mutual examination and reorientation the possible answers to life's deepest questions. The listener's task is to assess the teller's ability to adapt. This provides the foundation for plans for effective care which will meet the teller's needs and at the same time respect his values.

Obviously, no story has an ending without a beginning. The challenge for every story-listener is to provide every storyteller with the opportunity to begin. The stories told and heard in *Sharing the Final Journey* are timely and timeless.

May all of us wounded storytellers be so fortunate as to have a wounded story-listener with whom to share our need.

Dr. Glen W. Davidson is the Doane Professor and Vice President for Academic Affairs at Doane College in Crete and Lincoln, Nebraska, and concurrently Professor of Preventative and Societal Medicine at the University of Nebraska College of Medicine. He was the founding chair of the Department of Medical Humanities at Southern Illinois University School of Medicine.

INTRODUCTION

IT'S FRIDAY, 7:30 A.M. *Three friends are gathered for breakfast, a ritual which has become a significant part of their weekly journey for several years. Same time, same place, same menu, a few changes to accommodate cholesterol concerns or use up travel souvenirs. What do they discuss? Many things, mostly related to life issues: families, beliefs, personal experiences. One has a lifetime of walking with terminally ill patients and their families and has many stories to tell, but she needs the presence of others willing to listen and share.*

We originally had no intention to write a book. But it was not uncommon to share ideas and publications that reflect personal and professional interests around the breakfast table.

One morning I shared my story of the death of a very dear friend in Canada. I had walked this last journey with Jack and his family. What a gift they had given me. Sometime after hearing this story, Terry asked me if I'd like to co-author a book. "That would be great. But what are we going to write about?" His reply was, "It's time we put your experiences on paper." The idea for a book was born. Soon my Friday mornings were spent telling my stories in a more structured manner, with Jay's recorder capturing them all on tape for later editing.

We would like to share with you a few of these stories of journeys with the dying in the hope that they will help you better understand the emotional and spiritual needs of everyone involved in a dying and death experience.

Storytelling was a greater part of family and community life earlier in the twentieth century. When "the family" was primarily of the nuclear kind and within walking (or shouting) distance, people sat in backyards and on porches and the family's oral history was bequeathed to the next generation by story and yarn. Kids dutifully stayed at the holiday dinner table or followed adults to the "front room," even when talk of cousins twice removed seemed to drone on endlessly. But these would someday be recalled. And so would the "lessons in manhood" learned by a 12-year-old hiding behind the pages of a comic book on Saturday afternoon in the barbershop, drugstore or other gathering place, listening intently to tales of how tough it was in the war or the depression, or how Uncle Ed died. Then storytelling somehow got lost for a generation or two. Today it is regaining a significant place in the communication of important ideas and values as we relearn the art of listening.

This is not an abstract book about death and dying, nor is it a hospice manual. It does not use medical or scientific terminology to describe diagnoses, processes or theories. This is a very personal book written by three fellow travellers with a common commitment to the spirit (however defined), to the welfare of our fellow human beings and to the role and importance of family relationships.

Each chapter is the true and intimate story of the living, dying and death of a special person and of his or her family. These families have agreed to share their fears, stresses, emotions, joys and sorrows with you. We hope their stories will be not only an inspiration to you, but that they will convey the importance of truth-telling, listening, compassion and celebration in the midst of dying.

Throughout my nursing career I have been much more involved in the psycho-social aspects of care than the high-tech remedies, but I believe both should be integrated when providing care so we may give attention to the whole person — body, mind and soul. When Dr. Kübler-Ross brought the word *death* out of the closet in 1969, 30 years into my nursing career, with her book *On Death and Dying*, it did not frighten me. In fact, I was ready to learn all I could to become a more effective caregiver and teacher about this aspect of living. In January 1974, I had the opportunity to study at the first hospice program, St. Christopher's Hospice, in London, England, under the leadership of Dr. Cecily Saunders, later Dame Cecily Saunders, author of *The Management of Terminal Disease*. Much of my learning about dying and death took place in that clinical setting, caring for dying patients and their families; discussing experiences with staff on the wards; sharing life stories, eating, feeling, healing and growing in the common rooms and in the common mission. I observed the dignity and peace with which terminally ill patients were enabled to die, because of pain and symptom control, in a cheerful environment, with the involvement of their families and compassionate, understanding caregivers. I tried to adopt the hospice philosophy in caring for the families you will meet in this book. Randy, Jack, George, Nan, Gary, Esther and Ann — each of their journeys had a great influence on my life.

Norma Wylie

Norma's Story
Part I

The Gift of Tears

M y first nursing experience with a dying patient happened when I was a first-year student nurse. I will never forget it. One night, when I came on for my twelve-hour duty, I was told to go and sit with Johnny, a two-year-old, who lay dying inside an oxygen tent. I walked into the room with no instructions other than to sit there. I saw a beautiful, curly-headed little guy with his eyes open and trying to talk to his mom and dad, who were sitting beside him. I sat on the other side of the oxygen tent. Occasionally I opened the tent flap, touched him, spoke a few words, wiped his brow and changed his gown and bedding. But the tent prohibited any closeness between Johnny and his parents, and I don't remember us having any conversation. It was a very long time from seven o'clock until he died. Nobody in the nursing hierarchy came near. Oh, they may have stuck their heads in, but I don't think so. About two o'clock in the morning I saw this little fellow lift his head, look at his mom and dad and form the words "good-bye." Then he put his little head back and was still. Having never seen anybody dead, I really wasn't sure what had happened. I went out of the room to bring in the night supervisor, who informed me that Johnny was dead.

I don't even know when his parents left the room. The next thing I recall was being told to bathe this little boy before they took him out of the room. He came from a very poor family and his little body was not very clean. So there I was, left alone to bathe this little fellow. When I finished, Johnny was taken down to the morgue. I was given some other duties for the rest of the night. I don't remember what they were.

Looking back on that now, I often wonder why I didn't leave nursing that night. It was pretty awful. But I'd always wanted to be a nurse, so I stuck it out. I saw a good number of patients die "in the wards" but always tried to subdue my emotions, as instructed. Because I didn't know what else to do with forbidden emotions, I would sometimes run into the bathroom, lock the door until I'd mopped my tears and could come out and carry on. I did this the night I watched Johnny die. To have done otherwise would have ended my nursing career. It was constantly drilled into us that we could not be helpful to anybody else if we were showing our emotions. And so went the rest of my training.

No other experience throughout my training had quite the impact on me as little two-year-old Johnny who died. I don't believe my experience was unique. Probably every student nurse and medical student vividly recalls her or his first patient who died. But the impact of that experience on our later careers differs vastly. Each of us is an individual, bringing only ourselves and our own talents to situations we encounter. Whatever I brought with me that night, there was no equipment, only me. Certainly back then no one helped us look at ourselves as whole human beings; yet even then I was aware of my own sensitivity and sometimes overwhelming compassion for others. I really didn't know what to do with my deep feelings at times. I can still hear my dear mother saying, "Just try to understand Norma. She gets a little emotional at times." Mother was a very loving, caring person, but her German heritage had taught her to always keep a stiff upper lip and never show her feelings. And yet the last time we talked on the phone before my mother suffered a stroke at the age of nearly 90, the last words she spoke to me were, "I love you, dear." In reflection, I now believe it was on that night as I intuitively cared for Johnny and his parents that I began my journey to walk, unafraid, with dying patients.

The next experience that stands out in my mind occurred when I was a nursing sister overseas. I went over on the last boatload of Canadian army nursing sisters to serve in World War II. The scene is still vividly clear: a frenetically busy surgical ward with eight or nine young men, all my own age, who were dying. Some nights I was responsible for 90 patients with only two orderlies to help me. We'd make our rounds past their beds, giving them penicillin, and they'd say, "Sister, can't you just stay with me for a little while." I can still feel those terrible tugs, both at my sleeve and at my heart, because I didn't have time to stay. And yet these were my own fellows, my own buddies, dying, with nobody to just sit with them.

When I came home from overseas I was as confused as many other people were as to what this war had been all about. My whole value system had changed and I had no clear direction of where to go next. However, an opportunity to work in a veterans hospital in Calgary, Alberta, came along. It provided me with an opportunity to care for some of the returning wounded soldiers and to practice some of the basic principles of nursing I still believed in. I particularly remember one surgeon with admiration and affection: my good friend Smitty. I was the head nurse on his ward of 45 patients. He had been a surgeon overseas for five years and had cared for many who were wounded and/or died on the battlefield. Thus we could talk the same language and relate easily with our patients. Life and death were an integral part of conversations on the ward, as many of the patients struggled with their healing from physical and psychological wounds suffered in battle. The patients told many stories and grieved the loss of their buddies. Smitty was a compassionate doctor and understood pain, both physical and emotional. He taught me a great deal about pain control and how a sense of humor was a great medicine. These two vital ingredients for healing became the basis for much of my teaching with nursing and medical students for years to come. Later, they were essential elements when I became involved in the hospice movement.

During my time at the veterans hospital, I had many unforgettable experiences. We received visitors from all walks of life. One special lady who visited us was Eleanor Roosevelt. I had the honor of accompanying her on a visit and introducing her to many of our wounded veterans. Her humility, gentleness and caring as she talked with many of our patients and staff touched me deeply. I was both surprised and delighted when my picture appeared with hers on the front page of our morning paper the next day.

I enjoyed my role as a head nurse, mainly because of the staff who were committed to high-quality patient care. However, I had a yearning to teach student nurses and had received a certificate to teach in schools of nursing from the University of Toronto shortly before I joined the army. Thus, after four years at the veterans hospital, I applied for a position as an instructor at the Vancouver General Hospital. There I had an opportunity to develop my teaching skills in a variety of settings. I learned the importance of integrating theory and practice and found my greatest gifts were in the clinical setting. It was the beginning of many years of teaching in my own bedside style.

After nine years in Vancouver, a major change occurred in my life. In March 1959 the World Health Organization

(WHO) invited me to become a nurse educator in Singapore. This opened a whole new window on life for me, with much to learn. My first year of living in Singapore is a story in itself. Here I will only refer briefly to the topic of dying and death. The population of Singapore is multicultural. Then about 80 per cent of the people were Chinese, many of whom followed the Buddhist religion. And though there were also many Muslims and Hindus, all these religions were unfamiliar to a girl from Alsask, Saskatchewan, a town of 250 people. It was important for me to learn their cultural beliefs and practices quickly. Much of my learning was experiential, from teaching primarily at the bedside and from my interest and involvement in this multicultural country.

I soon learned that death has a different meaning in each culture and to respect this, even when the meaning differs greatly from my own culture's beliefs. I was invited to go to a Chinese temple with a friend whose relative had just died. My friend was born into a Buddhist family but was then a first-generation Christian. As we entered the temple, I noticed several tables with people sitting, drinking an orange drink and chatting. We joined them for a few minutes. Then we proceeded over to the coffin to pay our respects to the mourners. Some were crying and wailing, showing the expressions of grieving that I expected. But beside the coffin stood a paper house with toy-like furnishings inside and cars, gadgets and clothes outside. My friend explained these were all articles the deceased was thought to need in the next world, and they would all be burned when the coffin was removed for burial. Funerals remain an important part of the Chinese cultural life. Everything is arranged to ensure that the life of the spirit will be happier than it was on earth. I was privileged to be with a friend who was able to help me in my understanding of a ritual very different from mine but also very real and spiritual to these Chinese Buddhists.

During my second two-year assignment, the Singapore Ministry of Health was host to two distinguished visitors from the University of California at San Francisco. One was Dr. Helen Nahm, Dean of the School of Nursing. She wanted to learn something of the cultural aspects of Asian students who were studying at her school. The other was Dr. Anselm Strauss, Professor of Sociology. He was in the process of co-authoring a book called *Awareness of Dying* and wanted to talk with some Chinese patients who were dying. As many of the patients and their families could not speak English, I was asked to select an interpreter for him. Observing his interviewing skills was a learning experience for me. I became aware of communication, both verbal and non-verbal, as I watched the families and their emotional reactions to their loved ones. When a Chinese patient is near death, their kinfolk flood the space around the bed. Then one hears loud lamentations after death occurs.

Shortly after the visits of these two academicians, I applied for and received a WHO fellowship to study for a master's degree. I chose to attend the University of California because of these two special people I had met. I also wanted to attend a university which offered a master's degree in a specific clinical area, and in 1963 the University of California was one of the very first in the U.S. that did. I selected psychiatric nursing as my specialty, purposely to learn more about normal emotions (such as anger and sadness) and the art of communication, including individual and group counseling. Most of the students were much younger than I and still searching for their future. I believed I knew where I was going and had chosen this program to give me additional knowledge and supervised clinical experience to continue my journey. Changes are always painful and this was no exception, but the personal growth I experienced made it all worthwhile. One of the major changes for me was being able to acknowledge my tears as an asset, as a gift I had been given, and I was enabled to use them to help others in whatever way indicated.

Dr. Strauss was on the faculty and we were able to continue our mutual interest on dying and death. What a rare privilege for me. He continued working on his book, studying the dying patient and those about them in social interaction. Little did I know then what the future had in store for me in my journeys with dying patients and their families. His book, the first study of dying in hospitals, was published in 1965 and now has become a classic. I am proud to have had my own copy of this special reference book since its first publication.

Another outstanding pioneer in this highly specialized field of dying and death is Jeanne Benoliel Quint. She was on the faculty of nursing at the University of California at San Francisco while I was studying there, and she supported Anselm Strauss' research. At the same time she was engaged in her own research, which focused on nurses and their interaction with the dying patient. Her book was published in 1967. Although I did not participate in her study, I had first-hand information about it. Thus, my interest and knowledge in the study of dying and death was greatly enhanced by personal contact with these two special human beings.

Following the completion of work for the Master of Science in Nursing degree, I accepted another assignment in

Southeast Asia, but this time with the Ministry of Health in Malaysia, with headquarters in Kuala Lumpur. I had come to feel very much at home with my Asian friends and was delighted to be back with them. I felt I understood them better, having knowledge of their culture and habits, and we seemed to enjoy sharing our beliefs, special events and working together. The next three years were rich and fulfilling as we grew side by side. And living and dying were all part of it.

During my time in Asia, considerable work was going on in England regarding the management of terminally ill patients. The specific concern was the legality of large doses of narcotics for relief of pain. A young physician, Dr. Cecily Saunders, was writing in an English nursing journal on what she titled "passive euthanasia." She was also writing about her concerns related to pain control for cancer patients. I followed her writings very carefully to learn more about the issues and questions she was raising about euthanasia. It was the first critical assessment I had done of this serious and controversial subject. Thus, early in my journey, Dr. Cecily Saunders became another significant person to me.

In August 1967, I resigned from WHO with mixed feelings. It meant saying good-bye to many special people I had come to love dearly and by whom I was loved, so it was truly a time of loss and a time for grieving. I have always had difficulty in saying good-bye and likely always will. On the other hand, I was returning home to help my parents celebrate their 50th wedding anniversary, which was a great celebration. Both my brothers and their families were there, the first time in 12 years the family had all been together. We had a family dinner and others present included mother's bridesmaid, dad's eldest brother and his wife, and a few close friends. I will never forget the expressions of joy and love revealed by mom and dad at this happy occasion.

Living back in Canada after seven years in Asia required much adjustment, both physically and emotionally. I believe it would have been much more difficult if I had not been offered a very challenging position. McMaster University in Hamilton, Ontario, was planning to build its new Health Sciences Center. It was to be the first truly integrated health center in the province. The plans included a 420-bed hospital. I was appointed to the position of Director of Nursing and Associate Professor, School of Nursing. This made it possible to integrate service and education from the beginning. I began my new position in Hamilton in October but returned to Calgary to spend Christmas with mom and dad.

Christmastime at home in Calgary was the first I had celebrated with mom and dad in nine years, and it was wonderful. Little did I know when I said good-bye to them after Christmas that I would never see my dad Charlie again. On the evening of March 17th, a phone call from their neighbor informed me that dad had died suddenly from a heart attack. I don't remember much else, but I really didn't believe it. It seemed like an eternity before I reached Calgary, where mom and my two brothers met me at the airport. I knew then dad really was dead. Events up to the funeral are blurred, but then in the middle of his memorial service, when my tears were flowing, I developed a severe nosebleed. That had to end my weeping. In retrospect, I think it also ended my grieving temporarily — a physiological event no doubt precipitated by a psychological one, resulting in "griefus interruptus."

Mom insisted that my brothers and I return to our homes and our work, but I managed to stay for about 10 days. Then

I returned to Hamilton and became very busy with the McMaster projects. I can't recall doing any more grief work for myself until mid-December of that year, when dad's younger brother, who was a doctor and also my favorite uncle, died. In the middle of his funeral service I became hysterical — the first and only time in my life — and had to leave. I know now I was grieving for my dad as well as my uncle — two great men in my life.

I could tell many stories of the building of the outstanding medical center at McMaster University and the architects and people who built it. It was designed with the human needs of the individual — physical, psychological, aesthetic and intellectual — being paramount. Also, the family needs and nurse-patient relationship were ever present. I discussed with the architects the special needs of a dying patient, a sudden tragedy, unexpected diagnosis — all requiring the need for privacy during difficult times. Small, quiet rooms were designed adjacent to the nursing units, a family room adjoined the intensive care units and situated nearby was an interdenominational chapel. These were just a small part of what went into planning and building a unique humanistic health care center.

I also had the responsibility to develop the nursing organization. Because we had established early in the planning the interdependence of service, education and research, we were able to attract high-quality staff interested in new approaches to health care and the team relationship. It was an exciting time for all of us. I was privileged to be a player, a nurse who helped to mold the design and development of this innovative health sciences center. My role ended abruptly in September 1973 when the administration asked for my resignation.

Losing my job was one of the most traumatic, painful events of my life. Many of the staff didn't know what to say and so stayed away from me. Some sent me flowers, champagne, cards — but I felt very much alone. I was blessed with a few close friends who walked with me and comforted me. One of the consolations was that I was entitled to a six-month sabbatical with full pay. This provided a new beginning emotionally and spiritually. It led me into a new career journeying with dying persons and their families.

I had continued to follow closely the work of Dr. Cecily Saunders. Her long-time mission to build a special place to care for the dying came into reality in 1967 when St. Christopher's Hospice was officially dedicated. When it was well established, she developed an educational program for physicians, clergy, nurses and other health professionals. The program was one month in length and limited to six students. When I was offered a sabbatical, I wrote Dr. Saunders and applied to be a student. Fortunately she had one spot left. So, in January 1974 I was off to England for a month.

I arrived at St. Christopher's Hospice at mid-afternoon, January 6th. My heart pounded with joy and excitement as I slowly walked into what was to me a sacred place. Hospitality was extended by everyone I met, and soon I, the weary traveller, was taken to my room. I can still hear one of the staff saying to me, "You may wish to rest a while. Supper is served at five o'clock. The choir is singing at seven o'clock in the chapel. We'd be delighted if you'd join us." As I wandered into the beautiful chapel, I recognized Cecily Saunders in the choir amid staff and neighbors from the community. There were families standing and sitting beside loved ones in pews, wheelchairs and even a bed. The singing was glorious. What a

St. Christopher's Hospice, Sydenham, London, England.

gift to start me on my new journey. During my month I learned much about living and dying and how we can truly care — physically, emotionally and spiritually — for each other. I was also enabled to do my own grief work during that month. I needed to grieve the loss of my job — so similar to the loss of a loved one — and to say good-bye to my dad Charlie and my uncle Walt. I owe a great deal to Dr. Cecily Saunders and her staff. Working and playing together, I was set free to begin to live again at the age of 55.

I returned to Canada to make my home in Halifax and started a new job I had accepted before the trip to England, on the faculty of the School of Nursing at Dalhousie University. There I was given both a full-faculty appointment as Associate Professor of Nursing and made a Clinical Specialist in Thanatology in the teaching hospital.

I was anxious to begin teaching some of my new-found knowledge and experience from St. Christopher's. I began teaching care of the terminally ill to some of our senior nursing students and to some of the medical students. My position as a clinical specialist meant I was on call to any ward in the hospital where staff were having difficulty dealing with a dying patient or the family. The procedure was to go to the ward and help the staff and students interact with patient and family, using concepts and interventions we learned from Strauss, Saunders, Parkes, Kübler-Ross and others.

Having a dual appointment with the School of Nursing and the teaching hospital enhanced the need and opportunities for teaching at the bedside. When I received an invitation from the head nurse of an oncology ward to help her and her staff, I responded quickly. Most of her patients were young people terminally ill with leukemia. Among them was Randy, whom you will meet in the next chapter. Many of the nursing staff and students were also young and having difficulty in caring for these patients, as were the physicians and medical students. With the support and encouragement of the chairman of the Department of Oncology, we set up a program with the head nurse on that ward. A chaplain and I would appear every Tuesday at one o'clock. One of the nurses would discuss the case of one of the new patients with whomever was present — medical students, interns, residents, nurses and student nurses. The amount and quality of learning that took place for all of us during that period of time was astounding. I learned a great deal from the patients too, especially from my friend Randy.

As the nurses became more in touch with their own feelings and learned some effective communication skills, they in turn encouraged the patients to ask their physicians any questions they had concerning their disease, treatment, prognosis or whatever. Gradually the physician-patient relationship changed and open communication became the norm. The change in the ward environment was dramatic, with much more hope and living in the present to counter-balance the fear and despair so prevalent among dying patients, their families and staff. And what a learning situation for students! The chairman of the department became one of our greatest advocates. He and my friend Randy truly became "buddies."

I also developed an elective for senior nursing students on the care and management of terminally ill patients and their families. One day Cathy, who was caring for a male cancer patient, came into my office almost shouting "Help!" Her expression of soberness but with tears trickling down her cheeks told me she needed help. "I can't get him out of denial. He won't talk about what's really on his mind." I asked her to sit down and try to tell me what was really upsetting her. "Well, Kübler-Ross says the patient has to go through the five stages of dying, and denial is only the first one of the five." We talked about the meaning of denial, and gradually Cathy was able to relate it to her patient. He had unfinished business relating to finances and family situations that required his input while he was still able to provide it. For this patient at this particular stage of his illness, denial seemed helpful. As a result of our discussion, Cathy decided she could support her patient just by her presence and ability to listen. It certainly taught me to walk with the patient wherever he or she might be.

In 1976, I began to talk with some of the physicians and chaplains about the possibility of starting a hospice. I spoke to the director of nursing before we began. After hearing our ideas, she said, "We don't have any money." "Well, there are several of us willing to volunteer our time to try to start a hos-pice program. All we need is your permission," I responded. She gave her blessing. We had a team of 12, including a psychiatrist, two family physicians, the senior social worker, a chaplain, several staff nurses, and a public health nurse from the community. As I look back, it was a tremendous team. We worked for more than a year before we launched the first hospice program in the Maritimes.

The first hospice unit in Canada had opened a year earlier at the Royal Victoria Hospital in Montreal. Dr. Balfour Mount, a urologist and former cancer patient himself, had played a key role in its inception, development and growth. He had been to St. Christopher's just prior to my visit, so I felt a bond with him and his program. In 1975, while attend-ing the first international conference on terminal illness, held in Montreal, I spent half a day in Dr. Mount's palliative unit. I observed the total program but was particularly impressed by the training of volunteers and the role they played. I left with a copy of their training program tucked under my arm. We incorporated the same program in training our volunteers. By the time I left Halifax in 1978, the first group of volun-teers was ready to go to work, and the team was ready to hire its first full-time hospice nurse. The psychiatrist who was one of our original team members, became the first medical direc-tor. He gave a great deal of support to patients' families and staff members and taught other physicians about pain and symptom control and about dying with dignity.

As we were developing the hospice program, I also con-tinued with my role of clinical specialist. I assisted staff on any nursing unit requesting help with their care of terminally ill patients. I believe there was a new awareness in relation to pain and symptom control and how to adapt the hospice philosophy wherever needed. Much new teaching and learning was required, but it was rewarding to be a part of it and observe the changes.

I had invested a lot of myself during my four and one-half years in Halifax, in exploring and developing Cecily Saunders' hospice philosophy into the very core of caring for the sick, and in teaching and practicing what I knew and believed. One Friday in July, 1978, came my time to say good-bye to many dear friends and, to go accept my new position in Springfield, Illinois. I kept very busy with packers, movers and cleaning out my office. But uppermost in my mind was saying good-bye to Randy, who was not only my patient but also a very close friend. It was very painful seeing Randy — so frail but conscious — but he reached out and helped me let go. Some dear friends were waiting for me outside his room. They comforted me but also gave me some space and time to dry my tears. Then they came home to help me finish packing before going to their beautiful home near Peggy's Cove to celebrate the Halifax chapter of my life. The next morning I boarded a plane for Calgary to be with my mom. I left Halifax with many fond memories and mixed feelings of joy and sorrow.

It was difficult to leave the hospice program before it was really functioning, yet I believed we had built a strong foundation with a group of committed volunteers and caregivers and knew it would flourish. I have returned to Halifax several times since I left and have nothing but praise for the staff and the care they give. I know Cecily Saunders, who visited during our early planning, would also give it her blessing and approval.

Randy's Story

"Time to go, Norma"

Randy, a fun-loving 19-year-old, had started his first semester in college. During that time he became ill and was unable to continue his studies. He was diagnosed with acute leukemia. I first met Randy when he was a patient in an oncology unit in a large teaching hospital in Halifax, Nova Scotia.

I was on the faculty of nursing at Dalhousie University with a cross-appointment as a clinical specialist at the teaching hospital. One of my responsibilities was to work with terminally ill patients, their families and the staff. One day I received a phone call from the head nurse of the oncology unit, telling me they had a number of teenage patients who were terminally ill with leukemia. Her staff of young nurses were finding it very difficult to work with patients the same age, so she asked if I would come up and see if there was some way we could work together.

The nurses seemed to have difficulty with the doctors about telling the patients the truth. There was a lot of talk about treatments, but not much related to dealing with death and dying.

I told the head nurse I was willing to help in any way I could. As we talked, it appeared the best way to start was to set up a regular time each week to work with the staff. We chose one o'clock on Tuesday afternoon: one staff member would present a new patient and the team would contribute to the development of a plan of care. We also invited a staff chaplain to join the team.

I felt it was important to discuss our plans with the chief

of oncology before we began. We needed his support, advice and input. The head nurse asked me if I would approach the doctor, and I agreed. As I had had no previous contact with him, I was not sure what his reaction would be. However, my years of nursing and teaching had taught me how difficult it was for physicians to work with cancer patients and their families. Their medical training has been based on cure with little emphasis on care when cure is no longer possible.

Would this prestigious, highly specialized professor of oncology understand what we were asking? After several attempts to meet him, I finally followed him into an elevator one day and asked if we could have a brief discussion. I presented our request to him, and his comment was, "It's O.K. as long as you don't take any hope away." My response to him was, "If I do take hope away, I have no business being here and somebody better tell me."

Soon we began meeting on this ward every Tuesday. In the interim I tried to meet as many patients as I could. Most were in their late teens or early twenties. Some were married with families and there was a lot of heaviness in the unit. This was a new experience for me too, certainly the first time I had participated in depth with leukemic patients and their families. I was as scared as anybody but didn't let them know.

One of the first patients I met was Randy. He was receiving chemotherapy and was naturally very concerned about this illness. He also was upset that he was not going to be able to continue his education for the present. I asked about his parents shortly after we met. He told me his father was a fisherman in a little village about 60 miles from Halifax. Fishing was not a very lucrative business at that time. He had three older sisters and a younger brother. His mother was a loving, caring person. Although they were poor they were a close-knit family. When we first talked, his mother was also a patient, in one of the other Halifax hospitals, requiring knee surgery for severe arthritis, and he was feeling a bit estranged from mom because she was not able to visit him.

Randy and I contracted to spend two one-hour sessions weekly as "his" time. I was trying to help him sort out his feelings, what was happening to him, and at the same time trying to keep the staff informed. These sessions with Randy were over and above the group conferences we had on Tuesday afternoons.

When Randy was well enough, he would come around to my office on the floor below his room. Some days we would just sit. Some building was going on outside the office and he would get into talking about the construction. If we were getting too close to talking about his terminal illness, he scurried around it sometimes; other times we got into some pretty deep issues. We had long periods of just quietly sitting and it seemed we both felt comfortable with that. I don't re- member Randy ever getting up and running out of the room. It wasn't long before we developed a close relationship.

Sometime after that, Randy's blood count went way down and he needed to be placed on isolation and receive blood transfusions. I can remember going into his room and being very angry at the isolation procedure, where one had to mask and gown. When his father came to visit, there was no oppor- tunity for closeness between father and son, nor between Randy and those of us trying to care for him. On a couple of occasions during this period he was particularly depressed, even to the point of talking about suicide.

I took this back to the staff and the head doctor and told

them it seemed there needed to be some changes in the procedure. We were trying to give the best care we could to these young people in their last months, weeks and days, but how could families embrace with masks and gowns on? About the same time Randy had talked about suicide, one man did try to commit suicide because of the terrible loneliness and despair that comes with the isolation technique.

We discussed with the people in charge whether the isolation technique really made that much difference. Who were we trying to protect? Someone said we were trying to protect the patient. I said, "You know, if the patient's going to die anyway, surely some love and caring is going to be much more therapeutic for them. We also know that after 20 minutes of wearing a mask, it contains much more bacteria than if you didn't wear it at all." So we made the doctors sit down and really look through the patient's eyes.

We got the procedure changed. It was a kind of side benefit from all of us wanting to help the patients and families understand what was going on in their lives. Randy felt he had played a good part in that. Later, when he regained his strength, he was able to talk about how fearful it had been but how good he felt about helping to effect the change. Because this traditional technique had been used in hospitals for years, it was touching holy ground to even dare question it. So that was a big triumph for Randy and, I guess, a little one for me.

As time went on and Christmas approached, Randy's mother, a loving, prim and proper lady, was discharged from hospital. She and her husband faithfully visited their son.

However, I began to question who was telling who what. I found out the doctor had talked separately with Randy and then his parents, but they were not talking frankly with each other. Randy became well enough to go home for Christmas. He was excited about that, as he hadn't been home for quite some time and was missing his family relationships very much. I vividly remember his excitement about going home for Christmas. When he came back, I said, "Randy, tell me a little bit about Christmas," and he said, "I could hardly get back here fast enough." I was surprised. "Why?" I asked. He replied, "Well, everybody carried me around like I was going to break. They wanted to wait on me, 'Now you just sit here Randy and we'll get things for you.' Nobody would allow me to play with my brothers, and nobody would allow me just to be me. Nobody talked about what was really going on with me. So I've had enough of that. I'm glad I'm back." When he had come back he was angry because at that point he did not see himself as an invalid and yet was treated like one. He resented it very much but couldn't figure out why. "I'm O.K. I can go out and take Doreen out to dinner, why can't I wait on myself when I go home?" He resented his independence being taken away from him when he was still fairly able to be up and around. He resented being treated like a sick person, because he did not see himself that way.

Hearing those comments from Randy, I decided maybe it was time for us to do something else. I went to his doctor, repeated what Randy had told me and suggested it was time for a family conference. We decided it was time, that the game playing should end; everybody knew anyway. Then the question became who was going to tell his mom and dad so we could get them all together? I got that job. So we set up a family conference that very day. Randy's sisters and brother weren't able to attend, but his mum and dad were there, as were Randy, a special friend Doreen, the doctor and I.

The doctor began by saying he felt everybody needed to be talking about Randy and his illness. This enabled Randy to talk. Much to his parents' surprise, he told them how he had been glad to get back after Christmas because of what had gone on. After we had a little time together, his mother left the room. I accompanied her out to the sunroom. Mum had a real good weep. She told me she had been crying in private but hadn't ever wanted Randy to see her do so. That really was the beginning of a quality time for all of them, because the truth was out and the game playing was over.

Randy had several good months. One day his father brought in a big, boiled lobster for Randy. On his good days, Randy had a fairly good appetite. I used to make chocolate chip cookies and bring them in for him. He'd go through a whole bowl of them in the morning while we were together. It was easier for Randy and me to talk after the family conference. There was no more beating around the bush about whether we would talk about dying and death or whether we would talk about other things. It just depended on how Randy felt.

One day I gave him a questionnaire related to one's fears of dying and death with 15 items. The five that Randy ticked off were: (1) I'm afraid of abandoning the people who depend on me, (2) I'm afraid of making those who love me unhappy, (3) I'm afraid of losing those I care about, (4) I'm afraid of dying before I'm ready to die and (5) I'm afraid of dying alone.

Our own faith is often tested as we walk the journey of dying and death. I always felt Randy had a deep sense of his own Catholic heritage. In a doodle on the bottom of the questionnaire, he had drawn a heart and then written the word life beside it. Then he had drawn a cross that brought together the heart and the word death. Randy had filled out this questionnaire just a couple of months before he died. Maybe he was in some ways better prepared for death than we realized.

One of the great joys of Randy's life was a beautiful young staff nurse named Doreen, a very gentle, caring person with expressive brown eyes, jet-black hair and a trim little figure. She had just graduated from nursing and gave only high-quality care. Occasionally Randy would sneak his clothes into his room and take Doreen out to dinner. Sometimes he was out a little later then he should have been, but the nurses on the ward understood rules are made to be broken, particularly in a unit like that. We had to pay attention to the quality of life for these young people and make their lives the best we could. Sometimes Randy would tell me about the good times he and Doreen had the night before. The same day I'd also get Doreen's perspective on the story, so I was getting some helpful feedback. Randy got into trouble a couple of times because he was a typical 19-year-old. He went out one night with a couple of the other guys on the ward, and they all had a little too much to drink and came sneaking in like bad kids. They were never reprimanded. If I had been head nurse in the ward, I would have said that's fine too. But in many institutions, those patients would have been discharged.

One day Randy told me Doreen had told him she wanted to enter a convent. She was a deeply religious young woman. He said to me, "I can't understand a young woman wanting to give up her life for that, even if I am a good Catholic. Can you talk to her? Can you persuade her to change her mind?" I think they had some pretty heated arguments over this, because they truly had a beautiful, deep relationship. When Randy had more chemotherapy, he was very ill. His hair would come out in handfuls, and Doreen was always there to comfort him. Some days she'd be down in my office later getting her tears wiped, so Doreen and I became very close also. It was good to know she was there for Randy and he was there for her. She became very fond of his parents also. Her parents lived in a little village not too far from Randy's, so good family interrelationships were going on also.

In the spring of '78, Randy told me he would like to call me mom. I took it as a great compliment, but I also realized he had his own mother of whom he was very fond, and by this time I knew his mom and dad very well. I said, "Randy, you know you already have a dear mother. I think we better check it out with her." He checked it out, and she said, "I just feel very good that he can have two moms like us instead of one." From that day on I became mom to him. No one ever questioned this familiarity. We often get so protective of our professionalism that it has to be "Miss this" or "Doctor that." I never have been one to be overly heavy on "professionalism." I think you earn your right to whatever you get. You don't get it by status or by names. Randy certainly never overstepped the bounds, whatever they might be. I loved him like a son; I loved him dearly.

In June his doctor decided Randy could be a candidate for a bone marrow transplant. Because transplants were not done in Halifax, it was necessary to make arrangements for him to go to the Princess Margaret Hospital, an outstanding cancer centre in Toronto. It took a lot of cross-matching. It must have taken about a month for plans to be made. Randy was getting very excited about this. He saw it as another extension of life. I'm sure that when you are 19 or 20, anything that's going to extend your life for even a few months is worth fighting for. It's a very expensive procedure and his community took up money to help pay for it. The hospital was also able to get money from a couple of sources to assist the family with their expenses.

About this time I was offered a special position to teach at a medical school in Springfield, Illinois. It would mean leaving Halifax and, equally as important and difficult, leaving Randy. I told him I would likely be leaving at the end of July. We spent a lot of extra time together, sharing our thoughts, our feelings and our tears. He also knew his good friend Doreen would soon be leaving to enter the novitiate to begin her career as a nun — yet another loss, over which Randy did some necessary grieving.

Some of us on the unit thought it would be fun to have a party for Randy before he left for Toronto. Since my home was not far from the hospital, I extended an invitation and

Randy was delighted. We weren't sure whether to have wine at the party or not. When I asked Randy about it, he said, "Well, I didn't tell you, but a couple of weeks ago when mum and dad were here, we were over at my doctor's house one evening and we had a drink. If I could have a drink at my doctor's house, I'm sure it would be all right to have some wine at your house." So we had a staff party with spaghetti and meatballs and wine. We started at three in the afternoon because we wanted the afternoon staff to come, as well as the day staff. Randy was at his best that day and was a very cheerful person through most of this. Sitting in a rocking chair that afternoon and rubbing the back of his head, he said, "You know, the other day I went to my barber and I said you better be careful, don't clip too closely or you'll get a handful of blood." And he laughed as he said it. He didn't have much hair that day but wore a cap. It was a good party full of good wishes for Randy as he prepared for his trip.

Randy needed a nurse to go with him to Toronto because his condition was pretty unstable, and of course it was his good friend Doreen who went along. The hospital paid for her transportation and time. His mom and dad and I were all there early in the morning when the limousine drove up to pick up Randy and Doreen and take them to the airport. It was an exciting time but filled with anxiety, because in those years, transplants were not as perfected as they are today.

Shortly after Randy arrived in Toronto, we got word that he had developed another acute infection, was running a high temperature and had to be placed in isolation. It subsequently meant having to cancel the possibility of the transplant and bringing him back home. He was in Toronto for two or three weeks. I remember receiving a letter that warmed my heart.

July 2, 1978

Dear Norma,

That picture you sent me evoked many memories. I myself would have wrote earlier but some of my bionics were failing. And of course I was pleased at the party to say the least and if I have the chance to take you out before you go to Springfield, it's all set. It'll be my treat from me to you, and I'll certainly look forward to it, because you deserve every minute and more. Doreen got her treat, now it's your turn.

As you probably know, the transplant is off for now. The doctor wants to really try and put me in a good remission, possibly he says for even a year and then I would be in great shape for the transplant. In other words he wants to keep me in remission for as long as possible and then do the transplant. I have been writing letters all morning and my hand is getting a little cramped, so best wishes to you Norma and I'll be seeing you.

Take care,
One of your best friends,
Randy

Towards the end of July, Randy became very ill and we knew his days were numbered. He was no longer able to get out of bed. He was having a lot of pain. I can remember going into his room and listening to him just say, "Please take this pain away." Although we had him medicated, it was still difficult. He had pain in his bones, had lost his appetite and was an emaciated, dying young man. The last day I was at work in Halifax, I wanted to go in to see Randy, but I didn't know how I was going to do it. I had bought him a rose in a rose bowl, and three different times I started to his room, but I just couldn't get myself to go in. Then I ran out of time. It was 4:30 in the afternoon and time for me to go. I went in and sat on his bed. He sat up and put his arms around me and we started crying together. It was as though I was glued to him. I just could not move. Finally, he put his hand gently on my shoulder and said, "Time to go, Norma." And I left. The next day I left Halifax for Calgary. Three weeks later, the 16th of August, I had a phone call from his other mum to tell me Randy had died that morning. He had waited for me to go.

O'CONNELL- Mr. and Mrs. Charles O'Connell and family thank everyone who helped them through these past 13 months and at the time Randy passed away. Donations, of mass cards, Cancer Society and flowers money and food donations were appreciated. Special thanks to Dr. Ormille Hayne and all the other doctors, nurses and staff on 8 west floor of the V.G. Hospital and to Randy's favorite nurse Doreen Landry, and to Rev. Mackey, Rev. Granville and especially Father Rene LaBlanc, and the nuns, pallbearers, the music and singing, the visitors and especially Norma Wylie and Brenda and anyone we may have over looked. Our sincere thanks to all, in the loss of our dear son, Randy. MR. AND MRS. CHARLES O'CONNELL

Sharing the Final Journey

* * *

An epilogue to our story about Randy is Randy's story about himself. This was found in his locker after he died:

As of now, this book has no title because it has no ending. An appropriate title for this book would be the lives and times of a leukemic patient. Right off the bat, people say to themselves it's just a money making rig. I am sorry to disappoint you all. I want to make my point clear. If I sell any copies, 3/4 of the money will be sent to the cancer society and the other 1/4 to me. My book will be dedicated to Dr. Hayne, Norma Wylie and all my other super friends on the 8th floor, Victoria General Hospital, especially Doreen Landry. To name all the super nurses who pampered me and gave me really super care would be endless. Of course, you can't forget Frank Lo and Wendy Wagstaff who prepared a delicious Chinese meal and brought along a quenching bottle of wine. This is basically the prologue of my book and I think I will get into the writing of my book now.

Of course you have to pick a certain time to start the book and the appropriate time to finish it. I will start my book at Christmas time 76-77. At this time a tragic thing happened, my younger brother who is now 18 years old slipped off a truck and suffered a concussion. He was rushed to the Digby General Hospital where he was getting no better. Dad and the nurses encouraged the Doctors to send him to Halifax, and so he was sent by ambulance. The only boy's name he could echo was mine which was very upsetting at the time. I seen my brother suffering so bad, I begged the Lord that if anything had to happen, why wouldn't it happen to me. I was going to Acadia at the time and my brother recovered but slowly.

I went back to Acadia and found it very difficult to continue my studies. I could hardly hold a cup of coffee in my hands for a month, I shook that bad. One night I was approached by a girl who claimed she could read palms of hands ...

Randy and Norma
at his "going-away" party, in my home.

Jack's Story

"I've been waiting for you, dear"

NOVEMBER 1967: I will never forget this date because I was present for the founding of McMaster University Health Sciences Center in Hamilton, Ontario. My appointment as the Director of Nursing provided me with unique opportunities to meet the initial faculty and staff. One of those faculty members, Jack, soon became not only a colleague but a special friend. We shared a common love of teaching and had both specialized in the psycho-social and spiritual needs of our fellow human beings.

As our friendship developed, I was pleased to be invited to Jack's home for dinner and to meet his wife Ruth and three teenagers — Ian, Gary and Susan. Ruth was an excellent cook and I always enjoy a home-cooked meal. She was a very outgoing person. Jack was gentle and quiet, but with a great sense of humor. Jack and I would usually enjoy a drink and chat while Ruth was preparing dinner. He was an avid golfer and I enjoyed his stories. He also loved jazz and in later visits he often got out his clarinet and played for us. They were a special family and I soon felt very much at home with them. We had several happy years together before I left Hamilton in October 1973. During that time, I really got to know the family well, except for the eldest son, Ian, who moved west in 1969. Family dinners were always special, with Gary and Susan coming and going as normal teenagers. Ruth took it all in her stride, and I so appreciated being a member of a real family. Jack would share some of his research work with me. His particular concern at that time was the drug problems of teenagers, although for many years he had worked in the entire field of juvenile delinquency.

I believe Jack's great life work as an advocate for social justice, focused on youth, may have begun when he was very young. He was born to parents who endowed him with high moral standards through their own example and beliefs. An only child can be lonely, but this father and son seemed to have a special relationship. Years later it was still firm and healthy, as was Jack's relationship with his mother. Jack spoke so proudly about their activities — trips to England in their eighties, father teaching school part-time into his early eighties, and always maintaining an active role in their church. Because his mom and dad were living to a great old age, Jack felt his chances of living a long time were good.

Jack had a great ability to live a well-balanced life by combining work and play. He was very community-oriented, focusing most of his interest on youth. Ruth and Jack enjoyed the outdoor life very much and so it was natural for him to be involved with Boy Scouts and the Y.M.C.A. (he was a member of the National Council). Having been brought up in Christian homes, they agreed religion was also to be part of their family life and they were members of the Unitarian Church. Jack was chairman of the church board and also involved with a youth religious group. As well as I knew Jack, I rarely heard him speak of his achievements. He was a humble man, felt good about himself and had no need for public recognition.

Early in his career Jack had accepted an invitation to go to Flint, Michigan, as resident director at a home for emotionally disturbed children. This was a 24-hour duty and required living on the premises. At the time Ian was three years old and Gary six months. Ruth the true wife, mother and caregiver. She loved her Jack so much and was willing to go wherever he chose to go. From Flint they moved to Ann Arbor, where Jack became a faculty member of the University of Michigan. Coupled with his teaching and social work, his interest in research grew. Thus, in 1964 the family — three children by now — moved to St. Louis, where Jack was accepted into a doctoral program. On completion of his studies, he received an invitation to the University of Toronto. In 1969 he joined the fledgling faculty of Health Sciences at McMaster University, where he and I soon became colleagues and friends. Jack and Ruth loved their three children very much and had great aspirations for each of them to go to university, but they never pushed them and allowed them freedom to make their own choices. Ian decided to leave home when he finished high school. Although Jack and Ruth were disappointed and grieved his leaving, I'm not sure this was openly discussed with anyone.

Their daughter Susan, a beautiful young lady, had a great love for horses. She became friendly with a couple who lived on a farm and owned their own horses. To make some money, she offered to help clean the stables and groom the horses, which also provided an opportunity for her to ride. She worked on her dad to buy her her own horse, but no go. When Susan finished high school, she went to university and graduated in law. What proud parents Jack and Ruth were!

Their third child, Gary, caused his parents much anguish with his rebellious behavior. Although he was a friendly, likeable kid, he was also frequently in trouble. I can remember him and a couple of his buddies being caught trafficking. Convicted, they received a three-month sentence and were placed in juvenile jail in Hamilton. Jack and Ruth shared their pain with me, but, of course, did not abandon him. Shortly after they were released, Gary and his friend Ron decided to head for Florida. They had plans to buy a small boat after they worked and saved some money. They both loved sailing and planned to sail part-way around the world. Early in September they set sail with their parents' blessings. I remember getting a phone call telling me the two boys had been out of Jamaica for two or three days; Ron had been below deck sleeping and when he came up to relieve Gary, Gary wasn't there. I spent quite a lot of time with Jack and Ruth at that time. None of it made sense. They didn't know whether to go down to Florida or to stay home. They were in close touch with the police, but I don't think they went down right away. I think they were waiting until they got more information from the police, who had been out dragging, trying to find the body. Finally Ron came home. It was sometime later that Jack and Ruth were able to go down and go to the spot where Gary had disappeared.

When I would go into their home then, Jack would just sit. He was not able to talk. About a month after Gary's disappearance, their son Ian phoned from Vancouver to say he was the proud father of a little girl. Ruth immediately got busy and started knitting things for this new grandchild. I can see her yet, wrapping up packages and in her way saying, "Well, you know, the Lord giveth and the Lord taketh away." But Jack just sat in silence. He went back to work fairly shortly after the accident. I used to go up to his office — the door was nearly always closed — and I'd knock and go in. He would be sitting at his desk staring into space. I would either sit and hold his hands, or if he stood up, he would just stand and he let me hug him very tightly, but we had very few words during that time.

I'm not sure how Jack progressed beyond the staring-into-space stage. His research work kept him so involved that I doubt he ever shared with many people how he felt. He was a very private guy. He really didn't share an awful lot, at least verbally, with me.

Ruth and I had long talks, and she said she felt Jack was always trying to protect her. Consequently, even though they had a beautiful, close relationship, I sensed that they never did a lot of sharing about their grief over Gary's death. Strange how people can be so close and yet — maybe they just didn't need words, I really don't know.

Part of it was that each was hurting too much to help the other. Their son Ian was living in Calgary, and by this time Susan was old enough to go away to university, so there was just mom and dad left. Gary hadn't seemed to take life very seriously but had been a kind of carefree teenager, testing his dad and mom as far as he could. I sometimes questioned whether there was enough discipline, but only to myself. Maybe the two letters Ruth found in a trunk several months after Gary's tragic death tell a story in themselves:

Dec. 4, 1972
Hamilton, Ontario, Canada

Dear ?

How do I address a letter to myself? I hope this appears as funny then as it does now.

The main purpose of this memo is to present information for an accurate comparison between me, the one that is writing this letter and me, the reader. How will you have changed? What have you seen? What have you done? Where are you going? What is your future?

Since it is for you to do the learning, I can just try and describe myself, my being. Therefore, the following are points of interest to myself now:

1) Questions — *question everything. How can you question others if you have not questioned yourself. (It is so hard to find the answers.)*

2) Compassion *is of prime importance to understanding others.*

3) Learning *about myself is one goal.*

4) Love *is wherever you can find it. In its essence, it makes life worth living.*

5) *What is* freedom?

6) Introspection *is self-destructive if not coupled with the ability to see all the mistakes and laugh and accept them (compassion for oneself).*

7) Life *is a laugh.*

8) *I want to be young forever.*

9) *Are other people different? Am I different?*

10) *How do you divide six apples among five people? (That's the part about humor.)*

There is nothing strange about this preoccupation for my future. In case you have forgotten, I have just finished 14 months in abject poverty working in places like Dominion Glass, Mothers, T.H.&B. But it wasn't all bad because I had a dream. I pray it will not be a nightmare.

The problems facing you are still ones of learning and searching. What have you learned? Which of it was worthwhile? What can you teach others? And where are you going now? What is your dream now baby?

>*Humorously yours,*
>*Gary*

P.S.
Youth has been conflict looking for yourself in a world supposedly gone mad. Maybe that's the challenge. I am becoming a man.

Dec. 4, 1972

Hamilton, Ontario, Canada

To my loving parents:

This is written in case I do not open this parcel myself. It is to let you know how much I have loved you and the life you gave me.

Being of sound mind and body I make this my last will and testament.

I wish that any earthly remains be cremated and buried at sea. Any and all material possessions are left to my loving parents to do with as they see fit. In the case of my friend and compatriot Ron Budnikas being alive and wishing to continue our adventure I leave to him all my funds and possessions. To my beautiful sister and my troubled brother whom I worry much about, I can only pass on the torch of life and all my undying love.

Signed the fourth day of December, in the year nineteen hundred and seventy-two

>*John G. Byles*

witnessed by my own conscience and soul, as I cannot ask anyone else — they would think me mad at my age!

Soon after Gary's death, I left Hamilton to move to Halifax. When I would come back to visit, I was aware of Gary's presence. Beside his photograph on the mantelpiece was always a red rose. To this day, when I visit I take a red rose for Gary. Occasionally, there may be reference to Gary, but often nothing more is said. Ruth and I keep in touch with each other through the years by writing, phoning or my visiting.

Jack and I began to be more in touch with each other in April 1986, when he phoned me to say he was going on sabbatical. He had been invited to give a paper on child abuse at an international conference in Sydney, Australia. For a long time, he had been interested in studying child abuse in Asian countries, so he phoned to see if I could put him in touch with some of my buddies in Singapore, which I did. He planned to do his research in Singapore, Malaysia, Thailand and Hong Kong; visit a nephew in Japan; and be back in Hawaii for Christmas. Then he was going to do the draft of his book based on his findings from his trip.

In February I was told by a friend that Jack had not been well in Hawaii. As soon as they got back to Hamilton, he went to see his doctor and was diagnosed with a possible carcinoma of the stomach. I phoned to see what was going on. At the end of February he went in for a total gastrectomy. The surgeons found metastases, so the surgery was really only palliative. I phoned Ruth and asked, "Do you want me to come to be with you now?" "No, we may need you more later on." For two or three weeks I phoned once a week. I talked to Jack just after he got out of the hospital and he seemed to be doing well. By the end of March he seemed to be doing okay and was even able to have a few rounds of golf.

In May, as I was making plans to go to the Adirondacks, for some reason I felt I wanted to have a little time with Jack and Ruth. I booked a flight to Hamilton and called Jack and Ruth to see if we could have Sunday, June 14th, together. That was all set up in May. When I arrived at the airport my friend Jean met me and said, "You'll still be able to have tomorrow with Ruth and Jack, but it will be different than you were planning on." "Oh, what's going on?" "Jack's been in the hospital for two weeks, but they didn't want me to tell you. The doctor says Jack is dying." When we got into Hamilton and I phoned the hospital, Jack answered the phone in a cheery voice. I asked, "Well, is it okay if I come over for a few minutes?" "Yeah, I'd love to see you, but just give me a few minutes." When I got over there I discovered that he had wanted time to shave. He'd lost a lot of weight, and it was a great shock for me to see my friend Jack looking so ill. I didn't stay long with him that Saturday night. When I went over and gave him a hug, his first comment was, "I've been waiting for you, dear." "Well, I'll be around tomorrow and I'll be here as long as you need me. Goodnight."

Sunday morning Ruth phoned and asked, "Can you come over?" Naturally I got over as quickly as I could. Jack was having a lot of difficulty breathing. He had an oxygen mask on but was very alert. Without asking anybody, I kind of moved in and started playing nurse. He was very warm, so I went out to the nurses' station for some ice chips and put some cold cloths on his forehead. He said, "Wow." I said "Yeah, this is just a little bit of good old-fashioned nursing. Well, how about a back rub?" "Oh, that would be wonderful, dear." And I spent most of Sunday with Jack and Ruth. We called Ian to come as soon as he could. He and Susan both arrived late Sunday night. Jack, Ruth and I had our time together and that was important.

I wasn't sure what Jack knew. Knowing how quiet he was, I didn't want to upset him by asking questions. I suggested to Ruth that she and I go downstairs and have a cup of coffee. She said such things to me as, "I can't believe Jack's dying," "We've had such a good marriage," and "What am I going to do without him?" I just allowed her to have a good cry. When she had finished, I said, "Now, can you tell me a little bit about what you and Jack have talked about?" "Well, he hasn't talked very much, but I made him sit down and talk." She broke down again and cried for a little while, told me she and Jack had talked about everything, that he was prepared to die as much as one can be, and that he wanted to be cremated. Then she told me again, "I just want you to know what you mean to Jack and me with what you did when you helped with Gary. If it hadn't been for you, I don't know who would have helped Jack. He was so busy looking after me, and I guess I didn't do as good a job as I might have looking after him. So, thank you again." I didn't need it, but there we were back to Gary.

Sunday afternoon when I went back up, Ruth's sister and brother-in-law were with Jack. I left to let them have a little family time, and then I said, "Now, if you all want to go out for dinner, I'll stay with Jack." That was very special. We had about three hours, just the two of us. I tossed in a little back rub or two, and he'd purr and say, "Oh, this is wonderful, dear. You know, this is wonderful." He slept for a little while and then he started to tell me about his whole trip. There was nobody else bothering us. He told me about Singapore, about Japan and what a wonderful Christmas they'd all had together, how he'd got the draft for his book written and he'd sent the chapters back to get approval from the different countries. He said, "You know, the book's moving along." And then he said, "What have you been doing, dear?" I told him about some videotapes I had written audio material for and gave him a brief description of them, including each title. When I came to "The Cancer Patient," he said, "Well, of course, I'm not one of those." "No, you're not in that tape, Jack, but you do have cancer, don't you?" "Yeah, I've got cancer, dear." And that was the only reference that we ever made to his illness. We never once talked about the fact that he was dying and I never asked him. I guess I didn't need to.

I left him about eight o'clock that night. When I went over to kiss him goodnight, he said, "It's been a wonderful day, dear." I went home feeling, yeah, it had been a wonderful day. We'd had our own time together, the family had been there and I was able to look after him.

Monday morning Ruth called me over. When I got there I said to her, "You know, he's still very conscious, but he has this damn intravenous running. Ruth, maybe it's time to get hold of his doctor and see if we can't pull that needle out. You need to do it, but I'll go with you." We went and found the doctor; they wanted to wait for some blood tests or something to come back, but they finally said yes. After we went back up to the room, a resident came in with a physiotherapist, because Jack was having a lot of trouble breathing. His lungs were just filling up. I can still hear that resident saying, "Just give him a big whack on the back." I left the room, and said, "Ruth, you're not going to let them do that, are you?" "Well, what should we do?" "Get on the phone to his doctor, but fast." She called his doctor and then she went over to the resident and said, "Please, will you just leave Jack alone." By noon we had all treatment stopped. They'd taken out the intravenous so we could let the cribside down. We still didn't know how much longer we were going to have Jack, but it seemed to me that he needed some peace and some comfort and not all this other stuff going on.

Monday was a strange day. Although Jack was conscious, his appearance was that of a very sick man. I didn't want to be constantly in the room; I knew the family needed their time and yet didn't want to abandon them, so I just kind of came and went. I also was torn; a friend from out of town had arrived to see me, so we had a short supper together near the hospital. When I came back into Jack's room, the family was there around the bed. After a few minutes I said, "Well, Jack, it's time for a back rub." I gave him his rub and he seemed fairly comfortable. Ruth and Ian said, "Well, we'll just go for a little walk down the hall." And Susan and I were with him.

Just as they left the room, Jack put his hand up and took the mask off his face. I thought it was just bothering him. I ran out to the desk to see if they could get a couple of small nasal catheters, which would have been easier for him. I don't suppose I was gone more than a minute. When I came back, his head had slumped over to one side. I ran down the hall to get Ruth and Ian. They came back into the room and within a few seconds he just took a gasp. That was it, just incredibly peaceful. Ruth and the two kids were sitting on the side facing him and holding his hands. I was over on the other side, just being there. It was such a beautiful, peaceful death that you could hardly believe that he was dead. I left the room then, just to leave them for a few minutes with him. Then I came in and said my good-byes. Later I helped Ian collect his dad's things from the room. As Ian and I were walking down the hall before we went home, Ian said, "Well, Dad and Gary will be able to play golf together again."

I was okay until I got home that night, and then I had my time. Fortunately I was staying with dear friends who comforted me when I needed it. Ruth phoned me Tuesday night and said, "Well, I think we've got things pretty well planned. We're going to go out to the golf club for dinner tomorrow night, and we would like you to come with us." So the four of us had dinner at Jack's favourite table, looking out over the fifth hole, which was apparently a very difficult one and one Jack loved to play. I admired Ruth's courage, going out there among all those people. (They decided my name should be either Wylie-Byles or Byles-Wylie, and I was christened both that night.)

Earlier in the day, Ruth had asked me if I would speak at the memorial service for Jack on Thursday afternoon in McMaster's divinity college chapel. I wasn't at all sure I could do that; so I said, "Ruth, I can't give you an answer right now." Ruth said, "We've asked the rabbi, who was a good friend of Jack's. We also requested a close friend, colleague and a social worker to conduct the service." They'd also asked the Baptist minister who lived across the street from them with whom Jack used to have great arguments about theology (Jack's parents were devout Baptists). Ian and Susan wanted some jazz played as part of the memorial service. They also planned to have a short religious service in the chapel on Thursday morning especially for Jack's 100-year-old mother.

Wednesday night we went back to their house after dinner, and I still wasn't sure if I wanted to say anything Thursday, and if I did, what was I going to say? As I was talking to friends of theirs, I said, "You know, this has been a wonderful gift that the family has given me." The lady looked at me and said, "Well, what do you mean by a gift?" "Well, being able to be with them the last 48 hours of Jack's life, to have the intimacy with that family, and to see the very peaceful death Jack had, that's very beautiful. But Ruth wants me to say something tomorrow, and I don't know what to say." The friend asked, "Couldn't you just share that with all of us?" That, of course, was the answer.

I woke up early Thursday, mulling over many thoughts in my head. The word "celebration" was coming to mind, the celebration of life and death. That was what we were going to have Thursday afternoon: a celebration of Jack's life. We would have celebrated his death in the morning, and if later they were going to have Duke Ellington playing and a few other things, then couldn't I enter into that? I felt very calm after this and finally things began to come together.

On Thursday morning we went to the funeral at the little chapel, and as Jack was being cremated the service went on. It was quite beautiful: the organ was playing, and there were several lovely family wreaths there. The Baptist minister, who was very fond of Jack, spoke intimately about him. It was all a very close family affair.

In the afternoon as we went into the divinity college chapel, Duke Ellington music was being played. In the chancel was an enlarged snapshot of Jack playing golf when he and Ruth had been in Hawaii at Christmastime. So, Jack was there, very much alive, with his golf game and his jazz. Son Ian stood up and graciously thanked everybody for coming, then turned the service over to Jack's friend. The Baptist minister said a few personal words, and then the rabbi got up and eloquently recited some poetry. I can't tell you what he said, because I was sitting there thinking, "Okay, now, old girl, you know you haven't got anything written down, you've just got you, you've got to get up there and do your thing." And I did. Once I got started, I felt calm as I told my story — our story — and thanked the family for allowing me to be present with them during Jack's dying. I told everybody some of what had happened in those last two days, so his friends who were not able to be there would know that he had lived life to the fullest to the end, and that he'd had a very peaceful death.

Ruth had arranged a reception at the Faculty Club afterwards. A number of Jack's friends came up, golfers that I hadn't met, and gave me a hug and said "Thanks." I saw more men with tears that day than I had ever seen before. It was a wonderful celebration for a great guy.

Before the funeral I ordered a beautiful bouquet. Because Ruth and Jack loved Hawaii, I sent just a very small bunch of orchids and, of course, a red rose. When Ruth phoned me that night after the funeral she said, "The orchids are in Jack's study on his desk, and the rose is by Gary."

I joined the family, including Jack's aged mother, and close friends for a short time that evening. It felt good to be with them even though we were all very aware of Jack's absence. It was the time and place to begin to say a final farewell to Jack. The following morning I left for the Adirondacks to spend two weeks with other dear friends. They allowed me to have my own time for grieving and to begin to let go of a special relationship. The peace and quiet of the woods and presence of caring friends was healing.

I kept in close touch with Ruth over the months that followed. She had put on such a good front for Jack — the

*Picture of Jack, the rose, and picture of son Gary on his boat,
on the fireplace mantel.*

man she loved so deeply — during his illness, dying and death, and for her family and friends during the funeral celebration. I was concerned now about her own state of health. Telephone calls and letters helped both of us, but I also decided to go to Hamilton in June 1988 to be there for the first anniversary of Jack's death. Ruth wanted me to go with her to see the spot where Jack's ashes were sprinkled. Friends who have a beautiful cottage north of Toronto had offered to have his ashes sprinkled at the base of a new tree. Ruth and Jack had often vacationed there, so this spot seemed ideal. Ruth and the kids bought a special blue spruce and planted it there to mark the spot where Jack rests. I was deeply moved when she led me to the spot. The setting was so beautiful and peaceful. It gave me a feeling of joy mixed with sadness. This visit also allowed me to realize that my dear friend Jack was dead.

I cannot end this story without telling you about the birth of John the second. I spent Christmas 1989 with family and many friends in Hamilton, including four days with Ruth. Her daughter Susan and husband Bruce from Toronto were with us too. Susan was radiant in her early months of pregnancy and Ruth was already busy knitting. In June a beautiful nine-pound baby boy was born, whom they named John. He was only a few days old when I talked to Ruth. Her words were filled with joy but tinged with sadness too. "If only Jack was alive to see his little grandson. He looks so much like Jack." And Susan said to me, "I look in his eyes and I see my Dad." I truly believe Jack will live forever through the lives of his children and grandchildren.

George's Story

A Love Story

This story took place in Springfield, Illinois, and began on Valentine's Day, which is highly appropriate, for it is a beautiful love story. The chairman of surgery phoned and asked me to visit George, a patient of his who was terminally ill with abdominal cancer. He had already informed George's wife Marge and his four daughters about the seriousness of George's illness. This surgeon also told them he had asked me to visit them to help in whatever way possible.

The following excerpt from a letter I received from Marge after George died gives her perception of the beginning of our relationship: "It is Valentine's Day. I have gone to look for a chair on which to tie the Balloon-O-Gram George received from his daughters. I obtain the chair and walk back toward B607. As I approach the door, a gentle woman speaks to me, asking if I am George's wife. A beautiful relationship begins."

Marge invited me into a room filled with beautiful flowers and heart-shaped balloons. George appeared peaceful, lying in bed with his four daughters nearby. She introduced me to them as she hurried to return to her husband's bedside. I followed her and met George. I sensed some tension in the room. After a brief conversation with the daughters, they left.

George, Marge and I had no difficulty being open and honest with each other from the beginning. In fact, they seemed pleased the surgeon had asked me to come. They had already begun to talk about the seriousness of George's illness and seemed open to help so they could have as good a life as possible with whatever time was left. They told me the daughters were not very anxious to be involved in this kind of conversation. Perhaps that is why they left shortly after we met. When I left George and Marge, I felt we had a good beginning for the journey we were embarking on together. I was very aware of a woman and man who were deeply in love.

When I came back the next day and went into the room, Marge was curled up on the bed beside George. I sat on the chair beside his bed and we had a good, long conversation, talking about many things. They began to share with me, in a very intimate and moving way, their deep love for each other. They had been married 14 years. George was now 65 and Marge in her early 40s. He had been an engineer at Memorial Medical Center for a long time, and that is where he and Marge had first met. Early in our dialogues, they told me about their first meeting. Marge had been a dietitian at the hospital prior to their marriage. She is very vivacious, and with laughter she described getting off the elevator one day and running into George. He added, "That day I felt that maybe this is the woman I am going to marry." George had been divorced for some time before he met Marge, who was single. As an only child born to parents who were a little older, she said of herself, "I've always been kind of spoiled and I get what I want." And that's been Marge in the years I've known her.

George was only in the hospital about 10 days when his wound was healing quite well. He was able to tolerate fluids, was not having too much pain, and his doctor saw no reason for him to stay in the hospital. Both he and Marge were anxious for him to go home, and so he was discharged.

I continued to visit them in their beautiful home. It was always a great privilege to go into this home and see how Marge was caring for her husband. During the first few weeks

George was home, Marge did as much as she could. George was fairly comfortable sitting in his big easy chair and taking pain medication as needed. They had a deep faith and had been regular attenders at the First Christian Church. Their pastor was faithful in visiting George, and he told me they had meaningful conversations which always ended with a prayer.

George often used to say to me, "I wish my daughters would come and see me," and he began to tell me a little more about his four daughters. The youngest one, Charlotte, was only 10 when he and his first wife had separated. The oldest is the same age as Marge and lives out of town. Their mother lives in Springfield, as do the three other daughters.

By the end of March, George was showing considerable signs of weakness. He felt tired more of the time and was spending more time in bed. He continued to pine for his daughters to come and see him. The out-of-town daughter had a couple of children, and one daughter in Springfield had a son of whom George was particularly fond. One grandson did a lot of drawings he used to send to George and they were put on the wall in his bedroom, but visits were infrequent. As George became more bedridden, Marge decided she needed a break.

I wondered what I could do to help this family. It seemed that if George was to have the kind of a death he and Marge hoped he would have, it was important that they have some reconciliation with the four daughters. Marge had told me many stories of how she had tried to be the best stepmother she could to the girls. She had bought many elaborate gifts for them. I can remember her describing the Christmas prior to George's illness and talking about the gifts she bought for them and for the grandchildren. She was very attentive to all of their birthdays, had all kinds of family parties in her home, but never felt she had much affection from her four step-daughters. She couldn't understand. She would say, "But I buy all these things for them. George and I try to be good to them. We spend money on them, but they don't seem to appreciate it."

One time when I was over, I talked to Marge and George about the possibility of having a family conference and seeing if the four daughters would come over and be present around the bed with them. I left it up to Marge to explain the purpose of the conference to the four girls. I strongly believe when someone has a terminal illness there is usually time for un-finished business, mending fences and saying whatever one has on one's mind and in one's heart. In this family, I could see, though, that unless we planned something fairly concrete then that might never happen. Marge and George felt this would be a good thing for all of them, if the girls would agree to come.

I left it to them to discuss it with the girls. They did, and set the gathering for a Monday evening at 7:30. By this time, George was completely bedridden. He was still getting up to go to the bathroom but did not leave the bedroom. They had a lovely big bedroom. Marge always had a bouquet of flowers there for him and there were always fresh, clean sheets on the bed. She never left him.

When I arrived for the family conference, only the two younger girls were present. The other two girls had not phoned that they were not coming, but they had also not given confirmation that they would be there. The youngest daughter, Charlotte, had not seen her father for two years, so, naturally, was apprehensive. The other daughter, Yvonne, was a little more relaxed. Yvonne sat at the foot of the bed; Marge was very close to George; and Charlotte chose to sit on a chair by the head of the bed. I felt we should have some symbol of the two absent daughters. I asked Marge for two cushy pillows, which we placed carefully on the bed. I pulled up a chair and sat beside Charlotte. She didn't seem to know what to do or say. To sit beside her dying father after a two-year absence must have been frightening. For the first little while that evening she sat with her elbows on the bed but did not touch her father. They talked about a number of things and did some reminiscing about when she was a child. Yvonne, sitting on the bed, did some talking also. Marge was fairly quiet, and for Marge, a talker, that took conscious effort. Finally I was able to help Charlotte take her father's hand. That was very beautiful. She looked up into his eyes, and before the evening was over the two of them were able to embrace and share some tears together. Yvonne did not engage in that closeness with her father on that occasion but remained more aloof. Nevertheless, I think it was a good evening, and a lot of things had begun to happen that had not happened before.

The girls told Marge that after they got home that evening the other two sisters had phoned them and wanted to know what happened. Sometime during the week when I was over there, I was given this piece of information. I said, "Well, if you would like to have another family conference next Monday night, I could arrange to be here." The following Monday night I went over and all four daughters were there. I think Charlotte was the most comfortable of the four daughters, because she had really begun to open up with her father. She sat in the same position she had taken the previous Monday night, with the other three daughters and Marge sitting on the bed. There didn't seem to be any strain in the conversations. They talked about George's pending death, they talked about many things. They talked about George's grandchildren, about where they were in school. George talked about some of the things he wanted the grandsons to have. He was a great hunter and he had a special gun he wanted one of his grandsons to have.

When we left George's room that night, we went to the kitchen and sat around the table for a little while and talked. I had a strange sense that night that the two older girls were in a very different time and space than the two younger girls. George and Marge had decided they wanted to give each of the girls one more beautiful gift. It was to be a ring, with the same stone in all four rings. Marge went down and ordered them from their jeweler and an evening was set when the rings would be given. I was not present for that, as I didn't go over every day. I think Marge was rather disappointed in the ring giving, from what she told me. I don't think she got the kind of acclamation she was expecting.

Towards the end of April, George became totally bedridden. He was free of pain but required a great deal of care. He became incontinent and that meant bed changing and doing a lot of nursing care measures that I am sure must be very difficult to do for a man that you love as much as Marge did George. But she did them and never complained. It was amazing how she cared for this man absolutely. She'd never done it before but pitched in like she'd always had. The other amazing thing was that Charlotte and Yvonne took time off from work to help look after their dad. They did not want him to go into the hospital and he did not want to go.

When Marge was not attending to George's physical needs, she lay beside him day and night for the last two or three weeks of his life, giving him tender loving care. One evening she told me a beautiful story of what they had done the night before. They had decided they wanted to get married again. They asked the girls to bring in two little glasses of wine, to close the door and not to disturb them for a little while. Marge went and took out her wedding dress, put it on and went over and sat beside George. They each took off their wedding rings, repeated their wedding vows, put the rings back on and had their little glass of wine together. Then Marge took her wedding dress off and went out and told the family what they had done. From that time on, it seemed George began to slowly let go. He had the two younger daughters with him and the two older daughters visited occasionally. He was at peace. I never heard him make any complaints, ever. I'd go into their room, and Marge used to kid me and say, "You know, George always knows when you are coming because he always has a smile for you." I think he had smiles for other people too, but I did like his smiles. He was a very special person. We occasionally said a prayer together.

One night during the last week of George's life, I got a phone call about eleven o'clock. It was the only time I got a "come quick" call. Marge really thought he was going to die that night, and although we had made all arrangements for the funeral director she would call, and I had gone through all the things for her to do, I am sure it was very frightening for her. I went over and stayed the night. As he was a little better in the morning, I left because I had an early class.

Finally, the last day did come, three months after we met. I had gone to work that day, after phoning Marge and finding out that George seemed to be OK. When I returned home about four o'clock and called her, she said, "He has just breathed his last." I wasn't long in getting over and they were all still very much with George. Nothing had been done, and that was good. I think they needed to have that time to quietly sit with him. I was grateful I had this chance to say farewell to this man I'd become very fond of, to kiss him good-bye and then help with what needed to be done.

We went out into the kitchen to join the rest of the family. George had a sister and a brother living in Springfield, and a brother from California, who'd been in town for a few days. Although I felt very much a part of this family by then, I did not stay too long. I thought the family just needed some time to themselves. Marge's mother was there, so I spent a little time with her before I came home.

Marge had been downtown the week before George died to pick out her dress for his funeral, and all was ready. When the funeral plans were finalized, she phoned and asked if I would drive my car in the funeral procession and take a cousin and his wife who were here from Florida. So I was with this family all the way. It was a beautiful chapel service. When we went in, the casket was open. Marge had a red rose lying beside George, and I felt comfortable going up and again kissing him good-bye. I went back to the house with them afterwards, where there was a big spread and a celebration to say farewell to George.

What follows here is the remainder of a letter I received from Marge shortly after George died, expressing the warmth and compassion of a very special woman:

*I could write pages on your involvement with George,
the patient; me, his wife; and his daughters, but then
you know all of these stories. Why, then, am I writing? I
am writing because I wish to express to you a heartfelt
"thanks" for performing a miracle for George and his
daughters.*

*Our relationship, George's and mine, was beautiful,
but in the last chapter of that life together, you added a
dimension that only someone with your ability and
professionalism could provide. In the last few lines of that
chapter, there are memories of things shared between
George and me that warm my heart — things that were
so right for us, but things that I might not have done
without your gentle guidance and reassurance that what
"felt right" was right!*

*I have been reflecting, thus far, on how you helped
all of us. I would also like to comment on the strength
that George, the patient, drew from you. He was
walking a path that he had not trod before. You were his
guiding light!*

*Thank you, from the bottom of my heart, for leading
him.*

Shortly after George died, Marge came up to see me one
afternoon in my office. She had the most beautiful bouquet of
pink carnations for me, in a vase that was in George's room
full of flowers before he died. She wanted me to have it. We
were able to cry together that day, and I think it was good for
both of us. I don't remember as many tears at the funeral.
Marge was well poised, but I think the flowers, the vase and
the fact that the two of us were alone let the tears flow. I did

see her several more times, trying to help her continue the grief process. I must say she was not one of the easiest people that I've helped with grief. She laughed about it later, but with Marge's persistent talking it was real work. However, we had built a trust and understanding through George's difficult dying that enabled her to grow and heal.

In July that year, Marge, George's sister Mary and I went on a long weekend down in the Ozarks. I think that was a healing time. It allowed Marge to do some talking about George, to relax and have some fun. On the first anniversary of George's death I had phoned her. I wanted to make sure she was not going to be alone that day. When I phoned her, she told me she was about to call me and asked if I would be free to spend that evening with her. She wanted to take me out to dinner and asked me where I would like to go. Knowing that Marge likes fancy places I said, "Well, how about the Top of the Hilton." "Well", she replied, "that was George's favorite place." So, to the Top of the Hilton we went. She had been up ahead of time and selected their favorite table for us. When we arrived at the table, there was a little doll with a crocheted bonnet and skirt sitting in the middle of the table with my name on it. The doll was named in honor of her grandmother and George's grandmother. The card said, "Please take me home." We had a good evening that night, with a bottle of champagne and a delicious dinner. Naturally, we talked a lot about George. She told me about an odd date she'd had, and that George had told her before he died that he hoped she would feel free to marry again. She told me, "You know, I don't think I could ever live without a man for too long." So, I felt okay about Marge that night and did not see her but occasionally from then on.

I believe Marge did much of her grief work while George was living and able to help her. They had quality time, continued to do some celebrating and had some reconciliation with his daughters. He had also given her a gift when he had given her his blessing to remarry. All of this did not prevent the grieving she did after he died but seems to have softened the pain and the duration. I will always be thankful for the trust this couple placed in me, and for the deep, lasting friendship between Marge and myself.

Nan's Story

"Nearly me"

M y journey with Nan, and her husband Jim, began about three years before Nan's death. One of our medical students, Jeff, cared for Nan when she had a modified radical mastectomy during his surgical rotation. He also met Jim at this time. Both before and after the operation, this student was aware of friction and disagreement between husband and wife, especially related to Nan's surgery. I was working with the students about taking care of the psycho-social needs of surgical patients and families, so he was anxious to help them. At this time there happened to be a special event for post-mastectomy patients and their families about which I had told Jeff. It was to be a dinner followed by the premiere showing of a videotape entitled "Feeling Good Again," the story of five post-mastectomy patients who were models in a fashion show. I suggested to Jeff that he might wish to invite Nan and Jim to come, which he did. It was at this gala event that Nan, Jim and I first met. It had a special meaning for them, so soon after her surgery, and was actually the beginning of a long and difficult journey.

Before proceeding with their story, I want to introduce you to Jory Graham, the author of *In the Company of Others: Understanding the Human Needs of Cancer Patients*, which is her story of her struggle with advanced cancer and how she began a unique crusade to break through the emotional isolation surrounding cancer. Prior to the publication of Jory's book in 1981, the Southern Illinois University School of Medicine had invited her to come as a visiting professor. While gathering material for her book, she spoke with knowledge and conviction to the medical profession in particular. We believed our medical students, the medical faculty and community could benefit from this learned woman. Weighing less than 100 pounds and supporting herself with a cane because of bone metastases, she addressed a filled auditorium for more than an hour, permitting time for questions and answers also. I was honored to be her escort. It was at Jory's presentation that I first met my friend Lee. She had had a mastectomy and had come to hear Jory Graham's story.

Lee was to play a big role in Nan's story and our meeting at Jory Graham's lecture was the beginning of good things that followed. Lee was interested in starting a support group for women following breast surgery and asked me to help her. We were a good team, she representing the patients' needs and I the psycho-social aspects from an academic and professional perspective. A small advisory board consisting of an oncologist, surgeon, and minister was invited to assist in the beginning. Sometime after the group was formed, Lee suggested we have a fashion show, with the models being members of the support group. One of the teaching hospitals agreed to help with the planning and financing of the event. Lee was the inspiration behind it, selected the models and their outfits and coordinated the whole thing. The videotape that resulted was "Feeling Good Again", which explores the ways in which five of the women in the fashion show came to terms with the aftermath of breast cancer.

Nan phoned me soon after her surgery and made an appointment to talk about some of her problems. There was no need for introductions, because we had become acquainted at one of the support group meetings. I was aware of her extroverted personality and flamboyant style of dressing. Expensive clothes and jewelry seemed important to her. She was a person with fluid emotions, shifting from laughter to tears to anger frequently. She rarely appeared relaxed, and as I got to know her better, this was one of Nan's problems.

Nan had no difficulty in talking and soon began to tell me about herself. As a nurse, she really enjoyed caring for people but had not practiced her profession for a long time. Born out of wedlock and given up for adoption when she was a baby, she felt that she had never really belonged to anyone. She had married fairly young and had a son and daughter. That marriage had ended in divorce. Nan often used to wonder, almost up to the time she died, who her real mother was.

She talked a lot to me about her daughter Laura. I felt there was a fairly good relationship between mother and daughter. Laura and her husband Jim lived in a small town only about 30 miles away and had a son, Ryan, a few months old. Nan adored this grandson and always seemed to be buying things for him. She talked about her husband too; they had been married for 17 years and she was Jim's third wife. Jim had only one child, a son, from one of the first two marriages. I never met the son, nor did I ever hear Nan speak about him again.

Nan talked a great deal about her mixed feelings towards Jim. Money was extremely important to Nan. She loved living in the big home they had out on the lake, and she wanted worldly goods. Yet she craved a great deal of love and affection and couldn't understand why she didn't get them from her husband. Nan never seemed to acknowledge that maybe she was part of the problem. As she continued to talk, much of her conversation centered on material things. I tried to help her look at the problem this could create in a relationship with Jim. She sometimes talked about having so little money when she was young and now she wasn't ready to be separated from her fine jewelry, clothes and beautiful home. Nan seldom talked about her faith and yet she appeared to be searching for meaning in her life. After we had a few sessions, she officially joined the mastectomy support group and soon became an active member. It was helpful for her and gave her an opportunity to reach out to others. And we terminated our one-to-one sessions.

That summer she invited the whole group with their spouses and children out to her home on the lake for a picnic. It was a beautiful day. It was the first time I had seen Jim since he and Nan were present at the videotape premiere. Lee and I went together and were warmly welcomed by Nan and Jim, two very gregarious people. They had prepared a lavish picnic and activities for all the families. Laura, her husband and wee Ryan were there also, and so it was truly a family affair. After a delicious lunch, some went swimming while Jim took a group for a ride in his pontoon boat. It was an opportunity for fun and getting to know each other in a relaxed setting.

Soon after the picnic at Nan and Jim's home, I retired from the School of Medicine and made plans to leave Springfield for several months. When I let Nan and Lee know my plans, Nan asked, almost angrily, "Who will look after me when you're gone?"

She and Lee had become good friends and the three of us had dinner together occasionally. I replied, "Well, you know, Nan, you do have Lee and the support group, and you are a strong-willed woman."

She was also making plans for reconstructive surgery, because how she looked was very important to her.

When I returned after several months, Nan was looking quite well. Her reconstructive surgery had been successful, and she seemed pleased with it. She also told me she had undergone an intensive course of chemotherapy. She described losing her hair, surely one of the most devastating things that can happen to a woman. She was very grateful for Lee's help at this time, as well as the kindness of the other women in the support group who had lost their hair. They were able to identify with Nan in a personal way and had done some crying and laughing with her. Although she talked about the support and understanding she received from the women in the group, I can't recall her talking with Jim about the loss of her hair. To Nan, so concerned about her personal appearance, this must have been another factor in their strained relationship. Telling me about it after the fact, in her usual style, she was laughing on the outside but crying on the inside. Her hair had grown back and she seemed to have a new lease on life.

Nan told me she and Lee had become extremely good friends and had decided to go into partnership and form a business. They were looking for another way, in addition to the support group, to reach out and help women following a mastectomy. They called their business "Image" and wanted to sell brassieres and bathing suits called "Nearly Me" especially designed for women who had undergone a mastectomy. They rented a two-room office, decorated it beautifully and had some good publicity. Following an exciting opening reception, they were all ready to go. Customers were slow in coming at first, but they had expected this. They both had good business sense and tried to share responsibilities. But two unexpected conflicts arose. The first was Maggie — a

Wheaton Terrier, Nan's dog. She slept with Nan and was not very well behaved. Nan wanted to bring her to the shop everyday, saying she'd keep her in a cage. Lee believed that in their particular kind of business it was not wise to have the dog there. Second, Nan liked to smoke. Since Lee was a very understanding and forgiving person, a compromise was reached. For a few months the business progressed, and Nan and Lee appeared satisfied with their venture.

Then Nan began to have recurring symptoms. She suffered with nausea and vomiting and just didn't feel well. When she went to see her oncologist, the tests revealed that she had metastases in the liver. That was a very sad time for the three of us. By this time I had become very fond of these two women, and to try to help Nan deal with another downer was pretty awful. It was very difficult for Lee at that time as well, since she too was going through some tests to determine if she had metastases. I asked myself, how could I as a healthy person, try to identify with two very special women who had lost a breast, in Lee's case both breasts, and then faced the possibility of losing their lives? The only thing I felt I could do was just to be there for them. We used to go out for Chinese dinners, and I would take lunch over to them occasionally. Nan was upbeat, so we did more laughing than crying, because that was Nan's style. Nan knew that she could be open and honest with Lee and me, and so we journeyed together with our tears and our laughter.

Gradually, as Nan's cancer progressed, she was less able to go to work. To give up their business would be very difficult for both Nan and Lee. They had a vision and for a short time it was a success. They enjoyed fitting women with garments to make them look whole again. But they had to make a decision to close their business. They had put so much of themselves into it that letting go was a great disappointment. I, too, struggled to help these two special friends but knew it was the only choice. And so together they agreed to dissolve the business.

Nan was then spending most of her time at home, alone except for a woman who came in to clean and prepare her meals. I visited her quite often, but in the daytime when Jim was always at work. Consequently, my knowledge of their relationship at this time was only what I heard from Nan.

Nan continued to show anger towards Jim. It was difficult to listen to her ambivalence: on one hand wanting to live, and on the other unsure if that was really what she wanted. She wanted to leave Jim and talked about getting a divorce. And yet she took very little action towards that end. In the time I had been gone, she had done a lot of searching, trying to find counselors, religious people, moving from one person to another almost frantically trying to grope at some way to make sense out of what was going on. She discovered the Unity Church and said she found some comfort there. She didn't share that with me until the fall, when she became ill again, and started talking much more openly about how important prayer was to her. During that fall, and from then until she died in March, Nan often phoned me in the evenings and would say, "Would you just say a little prayer with me before I go to sleep?" She also phoned the Unity prayer tower in Kansas City, and seemed to derive some comfort from that.

From September until her death, Nan was in and out of hospitals several times. Her disease progressed rapidly. She decided to have more chemotherapy. So, here was this angry woman, ambivalent about living and dying and yet with a lot of fight in her — a very complex lady. Let there be no doubt about the fight in her. When she went back onto chemotherapy, it made her extremely ill, her hair started to come out again and she was generally debilitated. Give up? Not Nan! Her response was to get up and go shopping for a wig. She asked Lee and me if we would go with her. I had bought myself a wig many years before, not because I was losing hair, but just because they were kind of the "in" thing. That was my only personal encounter with a wig. I didn't like wearing it because it made me feel conspicuous. When Nan, Lee and I went down to the wig shop, I had my own experience in the back of my mind but certainly wasn't about to be sharing it with Nan. She was in a good mood the day we went. The shop owner, a charming lady from Korea, had a very good selection of wigs and was very patient with Nan. We had some fun, laughing and modeling. The three of us went out for lunch afterwards. Nan didn't have much of an appetite but tried the best she could.

During this period, Nan also let me see another side of her: a gentle, loving and child-like person. She had a beautiful musical teddy bear — Teddy Ruxpin — who sang lullabies. One day when I was visiting her, we were in the living room, with Nan sitting in a comfortable chair and me sitting on the floor beside her, holding Teddy. We listened to a lullaby as Teddy opened and closed his big eyes. It was very peaceful. What a beautiful gift she gave me. She later told Jim that Teddy was to live at my home after she died. Today Teddy sits in a love seat, with four of his bear friends, in my living room.

During this period, she and her daughter became closer. Laura was pregnant and Nan was overjoyed. She didn't talk a great deal about dying until close to Christmas but expressed a strong desire to stay alive until her second grandchild was born.

Once, when she was in the hospital and I was visiting her, her little grandson Ryan came running into her room and said, "Today, Nana, I saw a picture of Jesus."

This pleased her to think that her daughter was trying to teach her child about the Good Word. Nan shared with me that when her two children were younger, she had tried to take them to Sunday school, but they had drifted away.

This was the story of Nan's life: becoming very excited about something and then moving out, shifting back and forth. Laura and I became good friends. I had heard some about Nan's son Todd, but I really didn't get to know him until shortly before Nan died.

January and February were stormy months. A series of events occurred that were significant for Nan and her family and for all of us who were trying to walk the journey of living and dying with them. Nan was very open and honest, sometimes perhaps too much so. During her last hospitalization, I'm sure the whole staff knew about the conflicts between Jim and her. She didn't hide it from anybody. It was difficult for Jim too. He remained faithful, visiting regularly. He would phone and ask me what to do. I could do little except listen. About three or four weeks before Nan died, she was talking quite openly. By this time she knew she was dying and yet was trying to remain cheerful. She reminded Lee and me that we had often talked about taking a picture but had never done it. One day I took my camera along when Lee and I were going to visit, and asked Nan if she would like to have her picture

Lee, Nan, Nan's grandson and Norma,
taken in hospital a short time before Nan died.

taken. She was delighted that we carried through on our promise.

This same day, across the hall from Nan's room I heard loud voices singing, "Praise the Lord! Hallelujah!" A group of black gentlemen was around the bed of a teenage black boy, singing and praying. I stood there for a few minutes, not wanting to intrude but wanting to soak up the beauty of the event. I went across to Nan's room and said, "Nan, do you feel strong enough to come out into the hall and walk across with me?"

She put on her favorite pink robe, and we went over and

stood at the boy's door. A couple of the men came over and brought her into the circle. They were all ministers praying for this young boy. They put their hands on her shoulder and asked her if she would like them to say a prayer for her. This was a very spiritual experience for all of us.

A 14-year-old daughter of good friends had been asking me some questions about dying and death. I had told Nan about my friend Andrea and asked her if I could bring Andrea to visit if she wished. And she did. I tried to describe to her what was happening with Nan, that Nan was a pretty sick-looking lady. I didn't want to frighten Andrea and didn't want to force her in any way to go. Nan was very cheerful, which seemed to make it easier for Andrea to talk. We had a little visit and, while we were there, Laura and little Ryan came in. When we left, Andrea and I talked a little bit more about living and dying — a reminder that many 14-year-olds never have the opportunity or have never chosen to visit a dying person.

Nan had another unusual experience during her last weeks of living. We sometimes read about a dying person having a vision, yet we seldom have that personal experience where a person tells us of their dream. During a visit with Nan when she was having a great deal of pain but was very lucid, she said she had something to tell me. She told me that during the night she had a beautiful dream. "I saw two women standing on either side of my bed, both dressed in white and gently holding me up. And you were standing in the corner of the room looking on."

She said she had that same dream three nights in a row and after that she was no longer afraid to die. Her interpretation of it was that her two mothers, who were dead, were waiting for her and she was almost ready to go and join them. She told this story with great joy to a number of staff on the ward. It was a very, very significant vision for her.

The Sunday before Nan died she was very ill, hallucinating some and moving in and out of consciousness. I went to visit her, but when I arrived on the ward, one of the nurses told me that Jim, Todd and Laura were in the family room. I went to greet them there, and after a brief conversation Todd said, "I wish mother would stop playing games."

"What do you mean, Todd?", I asked.

"Well, she's never yet told us she's dying. We know she's dying, the doctor has told us, he has told her she's dying, but she won't let us talk about it in front of her."

Jim was fairly quiet by this time. I said to the three of them, "Would you like me to go in and talk with Nan? I can't promise that anything will come of it, but she has told me that she's dying. Let me go in and see if I can have a conversation with her."

I went in alone and found Nan quite calm and smiling. I went over to her bedside and gave her a gentle hug. "Nan, can you tell me what you feel is going on with you today?"

She looked at me and said, "Well, you know I'm dying."

Holding her hands, I said, "Nan, do you feel you could say that to Jim, Laura and Todd?"

"Yes, I think I can."

"They tell me that they need to hear it, Nan, that you all know it. Maybe it's time now to begin to level with each other. Would you like me to have them come in? I can come back in with them or wait in the hall."

Nan nodded "Yes" and asked me to please stay.

I went out and told the others about our conversation.

When we returned to her bedside, she was able to tell them she was dying, that she didn't feel that she had a lot of time left. It was very difficult for Laura. She was six months pregnant and was losing her mother; Jim and Todd comforted her. We stayed in the room for a while, and then I left to give them some private "family time." After supper I returned and found Nan semi-conscious. It really looked like she was going to die that night. About 9:30 only Jim and I were left. Jim, looking very weary, said to me, "I think I'll go home."

I said, "Well, that's okay, I'll stay with Nan a little longer."

While I was sitting with her, her eyes opened up and she said, "Will you call my son Todd, I want to talk to him."

I called Todd and he came in and said he'd stay with his mother.

Before Todd arrived, Nan and I had some special sharing time together. I remember feeling very sad and crying. When Nan asked why I was crying, I was able to tell her I loved her and was sad because I knew she, my good friend, was soon going to die and I would miss her very much. When Todd arrived, I left, still very tearful. I was grateful for the comfort I received from the ward nurses.

On the way to the hospital parking lot through a network of hallways and a tunnel, I began to feel the awful heaviness that sadness often makes us bear. Seemingly out of nowhere a familiar figure appeared. Walking toward me was Jeff, the same medical student who had first introduced me to Nan and Jim. He was a very sensitive, caring person and just the person for me at this difficult time. Jeff walked out to the car with me, gave me a hug and wanted to know if I could get home okay.

"Thanks, I'll be all right."

I fully expected a phone call during the night to say that Nan had died. But when I phoned the ward the next morning, Nan was very alert. Perhaps she realized she still had some unfinished business.

When I went in that day, she said, "I don't think Jim and I will ever reconcile things, but I have some things I want to talk to Todd and Laura about."

During the next four days some amazing events occurred. Nan reached out and asked her two children to forgive her for some things she had done for which she wasn't very proud. The second day she even sat up in a chair and started to eat. It just blew everybody's minds. She ordered special cookies brought in for the staff. She was never alone those last few days. Jim and Todd took time off from their work; Jim was with her mostly during the day and Todd at night. After Nan died, Todd told me it was some of the most meaningful time he and his mom had ever had together. They were able to tell each other they loved each other. A lot of tears were mingled with some laughter. It was a very special time for each of them. I had become like a surrogate mom to Laura and Todd, having spent a considerable amount of intense emotional time with the family the last week of Nan's life. When Jim and I talked, he said he had resolved as much of the conflict in their relationship as he could. He told me there likely would not be a reconciliation between him and Nan before she died.

Friday's morning visit with Nan was complicated by mixed feelings. I was getting ready to go to Mobile to conduct a workshop on dying and death. When I saw Nan, she was very alert. We had a little time together. She told me she was going to die that weekend. She asked just before I said goodbye if we could pray together. This made leaving that much more difficult. Before leaving for Mobile, I gave Jim my phone number and address.

Sunday morning about 6:30 I awakened and knew that Nan had died, but I waited until about 8:00 to phone Jim. He was so surprised to hear my voice and said, "What are you doing, calling me at home?"

I said, "Well, I just phoned to see what time Nan died."

She had died at 6:30. No explanations for things like this, except that I do know that there is a power greater than we are that intervenes, that sends us messages. There are too many similar occurrences to believe otherwise.

I phoned Lee and asked her to send a rose to Jim. Although I hadn't requested it, he laid it in the coffin beside Nan. When I got back and phoned him he said he knew that I would want to have a little piece in Nan's service, and so the rose lay beside her. Some of my friends, who went to the funeral, told me that there was a large attendance, especially of Jim's business friends. In talking with some of them following the service, they spoke especially of the many kindnesses Jim had shown his customers, particularly older people. Jim told me later how comforting it was to have them present to say farewell to Nan.

I went out to see Jim shortly after I came back and saw a very sad man. He didn't try to hide his tears. Nan's dog, Maggie, sat beside him.

Jim kept saying, "I wonder why she was able to tell everybody but me that she loved them."

I couldn't answer that for him. I think he knew that she was a complex woman, and she just wasn't able to love him, for whatever reason. But he never abandoned her.

Jim stayed on in the house. As the Fourth of July was

always an important holiday event for them, he planned a celebration. They always had big gatherings. Jim's mother, who was in her late eighties and lived several hours away, came down. He phoned me and said, "We feel you're part of the family. Would you come out and help us celebrate the Fourth of July?"

I was pleased to be invited. It was a celebration. Nan's presence was very much felt. He kept many things around the house just the way Nan had them, including Maggie. I think Nan's spirit will always be in that house. I don't know how it could not be.

Jim wanted me to have some of Nan's clothes. I can remember a strange feeling as I looked at these closets and drawers full of clothes. It was like touching something very private. I did bring a few things home and enjoyed wearing them but have often thought, here was a woman who had so many possessions and yet never truly found happiness. Her continual search to find out who her "real" mother was, was nearly obsessive. Jim told me that Nan had hired a lawyer in Chicago to open up the adoption papers to help in the search. They were never opened before she died, and so she died never having concluded her struggle to know. Not everyone can have a peaceful death until death actually occurs. And yet in Nan's dying, her family found each other in a new and loving relationship.

Yes, she gave them a gift, really. The things that happened in that family, and the things they described were very beautiful. Her second grandson was born a month after she died. I went up to the maternity ward the night Laura phoned me, about two hours after the baby was born. There was Jim, the proud grandfather, passing out cigars. He'd bought a six-month supply of diapers for his new grandson. He told me that since Nan had died, he, Laura and Todd were closer than they ever had been. And that the two younger people both see their own father, Nan's first husband, again, which had not happened for a long time. So Nan's death seems to have freed this family to find each other in ways they couldn't before. Nan had a way of controlling people. I can remember saying to Jim, and to Laura, "It almost seems as though Nan had to die to allow the rest of you to be free to love."

Gary's Story

"Dad has something he wants to tell you, kids"

This is a story of how I walked the journey with Gary, his wife Marilyn and their nine children during the last days of Gary's life. Gary, 37 years old, was terminally ill with an adenocarcinoma of the lung and had bone metastases. Although he was admitted to an acute care hospital at the onset for diagnostic purposes, followed by radiation treatment for pain and symptom control, when his physician told him of his poor prognosis he was adamant about going home as soon as possible. His wife Marilyn, a licensed practical nurse, was equally insistent about caring for her husband at home so they could spend the maximum time together. She was familiar with the hospice home care program and able to persuade their physician to admit Gary into it. This allowed him to be amid familiar surroundings and his loved ones.

As a hospice home care volunteer, I was asked to help this family. The hospice social worker had already visited them and helped by giving me the family history. She went with me on my initial visit and introduced me to Gary and Marilyn. Gary was in bed in a very small room. One thing I noticed at that first visit were all the drawings on the wall his kids had been doing for him. He was lying on a waterbed, because he had lost about 50 pounds. There is always the danger of pressure sores developing with bedridden patients who have lost weight. Gary also had bone metastases, which can be very painful. I think Marilyn was trying to do everything she possibly could to keep her husband comfortable.

I asked them a little bit about themselves, because I was curious where all these nine kids had come from with such a young mom and dad. They told me this was a second marriage for both of them. Marilyn had brought six children. Her youngest, Charlie, was seven, and her oldest, Angie, 18. Gary had brought three children from his first marriage — ages eight, 13 and 14. None of them were home that day. I appreciated that, because it gave me a chance to get to know Marilyn and Gary. He was very lucid and seemed to want to talk. He had an oxygen tank by the bed but was not using his mask while I was there. In the course of our conversation, I asked them how much talking they were doing with each other about his illness. I let them know I had been given some medical history around his diagnosis. I asked if they understood that when they had agreed to go into a hospice program, it meant that at least the physician had discussed with them the fact that Gary was terminally ill. They both looked at me a little strangely and said, "You know, we've just begun to talk, really talk, but we're so glad we have." Gary said, "We were playing games with each other, and we weren't being open and honest. We were very abrupt and irritable, but all of that has stopped since we have kind of made a truce that we were going to be open and honest with each other."

Their answer also gave me a chance to ask them what the kids knew. They said, "We really haven't told them very much yet. They know that their dad is very sick." Gary was on a fair amount of morphine, but that did not seem to be controlling his pain as much as one would have liked. He told me he often found it difficult to hide his pain when the kids came home. During that first visit, I talked with them for about an hour before I suggested that they may want to think about telling the kids. I said, "It's your choice. I can't do it for you, but whenever you choose to do it, I can be there to help you in any way you want me to."

Our journey together began that day. I guess I was there two hours. We just took our time. Gary told me a little about himself. He had been a truck driver for 17 years. His father was a farmer and had three sons. I'm not sure when Gary became ill, but at some point his father had lost his farm. With no other occupation, his father had gone into truck driving and his three sons had followed suit. Gary went on, quite willing to talk. When I asked him about his eating and sleeping patterns, he said, "Well, you know, I've been a truck driver for 17 years, and I usually drove at night. It's been kind of hard to change that sleeping pattern around. When I was driving, one of the things that I found was necessary to stay awake at night was to smoke." Gary was well aware of his heavy smoking as being one of the likely causes of his present illness, and felt sad that it was too late to change that.

When I left Gary, I told him I would get in touch with his doctor to see if something could be done to increase his pain medication. One of the great benefits of hospice home care is that the patient and family have immediate access to whoever is in the care system. Marilyn seemed reluctant to call, so I said I would do it for them. A couple of days after I made my initial visit, Gary was readmitted to the hospice unit with the understanding that he would only be there for a few days to bring his pain under control. He was very reluctant about going. I think he was afraid he'd never get back home. After he was admitted and I went to see him, Marilyn told me that to get him there she really had to take over, saying, "Come on, Gary, we're going, and we will get you home as quickly as we can." So I picked up that there was a beautiful relationship between this man and woman.

I went back to see Gary the next day, and he was already

saying, "Hurry up and get this medication under control so I can go home." When I went in, his 13-year-old son Jeremy was sitting beside him. After Jeremy left, Gary was talking about his son and said, "I am very concerned about Jeremy because he tries to skip school and doesn't work very hard." Gary went on, "If there's anything good about me being ill, it's that Jeremy says, 'Well, dad, I see more of you now and I will try to do better at school.'" Gary told me that Marilyn had some conferences with the teacher, and that Jeremy really was becoming quite a problem kid and he really wanted his dad at home more. When Gary was driving, he would be gone six weeks at a time, so for a good part of the time Marilyn was both mother and father to these nine kids.

The second day Gary was in, he had morphine running intravenously to try to give him more even control of his pain. When I went back in, Marilyn was there, and they both said to me, "We would like to tell the kids, we think the time has come." They both seemed to have an apprehension of running out of time. Gary talked very openly that day about wanting to tell his kids. I noticed that he had a number of hasty notes, and I asked, "What are you doing, Gary?" "Well, I'm writing a special little message to each of my daughters to be sealed and given to them after I die. You know, I don't have many worldly goods, but I've got a special belt," and he also named two or three other special things. "I've marked on each of these which one of my sons is to get my belt, and who's to get my Harley-Davidson shirt and who's to get my bandanna." Those were his worldly goods, at least the ones he cared about, and he was feeling okay about that.

At that time we also talked about the possibility of doing some kind of videotape. He wanted to leave a message on tape as well as in writing, but also decided that he wasn't quite well enough to do that yet. As Gary and Marilyn began to talk, and as I listened to them, it seemed that the top priority was to tell the kids. So they arranged, a day or two later, to have all nine kids in the room. I said, "Okay, I will be there." I remember going in an hour or so before the time set for this event, sitting down with Gary again and saying, "You know, Gary, you need to tell me what you want me to do, but more important, what are you going to do?" "Well, I would like to start and tell them as much as I can, but if I get stuck..." I said, "Yeah, okay, if you get stuck I'll try to fill in."

The kids began to arrive. It was an unforgettable scene. Marilyn was at the head of the bed on the left-hand side, the nine kids on or around the bed, and Gary's mother was sitting at the foot of the bed. On his right side, where the intravenous was running, was Marilyn's little boy Charlie. Charlie loved his stepfather dearly. He crawled up onto the bed and was tucked under Gary's right arm. Gary's youngest girl, Jennifer, a little thing with great big glasses that were too big for her little face, crawled up on the other side and was lying with Gary's left arm tucked around her. Mike, an 11-year-old, was sitting in Gary's wheelchair by himself. Jeremy was standing over near the corner of the room, alone. The rest of them were all around. I was leaning against the empty bed in the room with two or three of the kids sitting on the bed. Gary sat up fairly straight in bed and said, "Dad has something he wants to tell you, kids. I just want to let you know that your dad is dying." There were shouts, screams, tears, silence and a great mixture of emotions. Gary sat there very quietly. Marilyn tried to comfort the kids around her, and I tried to get my arms around a few of them. Mike, sitting over in the wheelchair, was looking very alone. I found out later that Mike has had severe migraines since he was a little boy. Jeremy was the one I was most concerned about. I went over to him, but he was just wanting to do this by himself.

Finally, with some tears wiped away and some still coming down, Gary looked at the kids again and said, "You know, your Dad has never been much of a religious guy, but many nights when I was driving alone in the truck I prayed, and I want you kids to know that. Now I'm asking you if you will pray for me, because I'm going to need all the help I can get from you." I can't remember everything that went on after that. I think I became somewhat numbed with it all. Gary was being so strong, so brave in his telling. Grandmother went out of the room with a couple of the kids with her. I spent a little time with Gary and Marilyn, and then asked them if they wanted to be alone. I left the room with some of the kids. The staff in the ward knew what was happening and gathered around to comfort and care for the kids. They moved back and forth helping each other. It was a tremendously moving experience, one I will never forget.

I came to love this family. Some health professionals will argue that you cannot be objective in your caregiving if you become involved. I would argue that you can't give total care if you don't get involved. If you're feeling, and if you're going to use your feelings as part of the therapeutic process, you can't pretend they don't exist. If I hadn't been there, I'm not sure that family conference would ever have happened. Gary and Marilyn may have told the kids, but they may have been too scared to do it alone. It is a very difficult and very courageous thing for anybody to do. I like to believe that I didn't do much except be there. Gary said afterwards it was very helpful just knowing I was there to help pick up some of the pieces as he was telling them.

It's well documented by many people that unless you have mutual communication between the caregiver and those receiving the care, then you do not give quality care, and the person dies with all kinds of "if onlys" being raised by the family: "If only we had talked to Dad about this," or "If only we had told Dad a few more times we loved him," or whatever. After Gary died, I never once heard that expression, "If only." They had done their work. I believe more and more that it doesn't take away the grieving process, but it lessens the intensity of it. The family was doing its anticipatory grief, and Gary was helping them with it. Gary gave a powerful demonstration that the dying person gives gifts and provides strength to enable the family to do its grief work.

I was trying to figure out who was supporting Marilyn. Gary's mother, Peggy, was always sitting in Gary and Marilyn's home but found it difficult to become involved. Gary's father and two brothers were on the road driving their trucks. The oldest daughter, Angie, was willing to help but needed assistance. I gave her a book to read, *The Land Beyond Tears*, by Barry Neil Kaufman and Suzi Lyte Kaufman, the story of a 17-year-old boy, Sam, and his family facing the death of their mother. In the book no one was really willing to talk about her dying until Sam agreed to receive help from a grief counselor. Sam learned how to accept what was happening and taught his family to cope. Angie found the book helpful, and she became the support Marilyn needed.

Before Gary went home, arrangements were made to deliver an electric bed to his home. However, the rental of special equipment plus medication for pain and symptom control can place a financial burden on a family. Marilyn became very concerned about how she would be able to feed her large family, let alone pay the bills. She had quit her hospital job as a LPN to spend time caring for Gary, and Gary's income had ceased some months before. She needed special papers signed in order to be eligible for aid from social services. Her emotions and frustrations became acute, "What can I do? Who will help me?" I was able to contact the hospice social worker, who came to Marilyn's rescue and arranged to get some money coming in to this family.

So here's this big family all at home, and each one wanting some special time with Dad before he died. His condition deteriorated much more quickly than any of them had expected, I think, although to look at Gary he certainly had all the appearances of a dying man. The kids were marvelous in how they worked out how each would have their own special time with dad. They said to Marilyn, "Could we work out a roster, and each stay home from school for one day alone with dad?" Little Charlie kind of snuck in and had extra time. From what Marilyn tells me, Charlie's own father had not been a very good father to him, but Charlie just worshiped Gary. Charlie spent many hours, day and night, just quietly being present. I would see him at the head of the bed, on top of the bed and at times under the covers to be as close as he could. I'm sure he respected the other kids needing their time with their dad also. They all did have their own day at home, to sit with dad, do some of the caring, to help turn him and just be there.

One day Marilyn phoned to tell me she had decided it was time to go to the funeral home to make plans for Gary's funeral. She wasn't quite sure how she was going to get through that. Gary was having extra pain, and I think she was caught, not wanting to leave him alone even long enough to go to the funeral home and very worried about his extra pain. By this time, Gary was not able to take liquid morphine. We got an order for morphine suppositories, which were enough to ease the pain. That allowed Marilyn to proceed with funeral plans. Angie and her boyfriend agreed to go to the funeral home with her. This task was not only difficult for Marilyn but very painful for Angie. She and her boyfriend were making plans to be married several months later. Although Gary was her step-dad, they had a very close relationship. Gary had not been so ill when Angie first talked about marriage plans, and Angie had very much wanted him to give her away. Even at this stage of Gary's illness, Angie said, "I wish dad could live long enough to give me away."

Early in my relationship with this family, we discussed the possibility of doing a videotape as a permanent visual remembrance of time spent together as a family. They savoured the idea, but when attempts were made for the actual taping, Gary's condition was too poor to go through with it. As his illness progressed we talked about taking a family picture. Marilyn said they had never had one taken. I said, "Well, if Gary gets well enough again, we'll arrange to have one taken." Picture-taking often is one way of helping the family cope during the dying process. The timing was crucial, as Gary was becoming weaker and less responsive. It was important that Marilyn let me know when we should take the picture so we would not intrude on their privacy.

Gary's two brothers and his dad were coming home for the weekend. Marilyn was excited that they were coming, and yet she was very sad because Gary was not responding. The two brothers had not seen Gary for quite some time, and I think Marilyn was wanting to protect them. These three brothers had a very special, close relationship: three great big guys, each over six feet tall, weighing over 200 pounds and, along with their dad, all truck drivers. I said, "Well, let's just keep in close touch by the phone, and if Gary begins to respond, let me know quickly and we can go out and take some pictures." On Sunday morning Marilyn phoned me, and she was as high as a kite. "Gary sat up in bed this morning, and he's talking with his brothers, and it's just beautiful, it's just beautiful! He talked with everyone." She said they talked about all kinds of things they had never talked about before. There was a period when the kids left the room and left the three brothers together with their dad.

I agreed we would go out Monday night to take pictures. Two photographers and I went with all our camera paraphernalia, only to find that Gary was only semi-conscious. When I went in and I met these two big, handsome brothers sitting in chairs crying — it was a moving scene. They couldn't believe that their brother was dying, and their conversation stuck on, "But he's so young, so young." Their wives, mom and grandmother were all there too. With everybody there and my two photographer friends and I trying to get into this tiny bedroom with some camera equipment, I had ambivalent feelings: I wanted to be there but didn't want to be there, wanted to give them a family photo but didn't want to intrude on their family privacy as Gary was dying. I wondered whether we should just take our equipment and go home. I checked it out with Marilyn, and she said, "No, would you please take the pictures." That young woman then courageously orchestrated who was to have their pictures taken. Gary's mom and dad would not come into the picture, nor would grandma, but they certainly didn't object to the picture-taking. I think they really had great respect for Marilyn and how she was handling it. And those nine kids were wonderfully strong again as they gathered around dad's bed.

After the family picture had been taken, the two brothers wanted their picture taken with Gary. That was another moving experience, to see a brother on each side of Gary, hugging him. Then Marilyn wanted her own pictures with her husband. It was quite an evening. Brian and Gary (the photographers) and I left shortly after we took the pictures. We sat silently in the car until I said, "Well, do you guys want to come to my house for a little drink?" Brian said, "I need to." We shed our own tears and did a bit of our own processing. That was very important for all of us.

First thing Wednesday morning I got a phone call from the hospice counselor to tell me that Gary had died at 2:30 that morning. And that's when my time to fall apart came; I think I'd been pretty tough up to that point. I can remember Elizabeth, a nurse friend, coming over. I don't know how she knew I needed her that morning, maybe she'd come to do something, but whatever she was going to do, I needed her. I felt very sad and cried and cried. Some of my tears were those of grief — the death of such a young man, Marilyn's despair and empathy for all the kids. But I also felt anger at the way the "red tape" in our social and health care systems had made Gary's dying even harder for Marilyn.

The next day I wanted to go out and see the family. I didn't want to go alone, so I asked my good friend Ahbee, the hospice counselor, to go with me. When we got to the house, little Mike answered the door and I asked the kids where their mom was and they said, "She's curled up on dad's bed." I can remember going into the bedroom quietly, with the kids now caring for mom. It was very beautiful to see how suddenly mom needed caring for and the kids were there to do it, all nine of them.

Brian developed the pictures very quickly. That was need for another trip out to show the family the pictures, and we all had a cry together. I can remember being very cautious about showing the pictures, because I wasn't sure how the kids were going to react to the sight of their father. In the pictures, Gary certainly has all the appearances of a dying man, and yet they never expressed that. They were just joyous to have a family picture — the only one they have. It has since been enlarged and sits in their living room. As I look at my copy of this picture, the kid I got closest to was Michael, then a chubby little guy. Whenever I would phone, Michael was always on the line and would say, "Yeah, Norma, how are you today?" Or he was there to open the door and became the host of the family. Overweight and beset by migraines, and yet he was just a dear, dear kid. Once Michael would give me a hug, then the other kids would gather round, so I got lots of hugs from these kids, especially the boys.

Well, that was the end of February. I could not go to the funeral because I was out of town. Marilyn and Gary did not affiliate with any particular church, but Marilyn was a Catholic and had tried to bring her children up Catholic. In a nominal way she always stayed within the Catholic faith, and so Gary had a Catholic funeral. Marilyn didn't talk a great deal about it, and I did not see her for a couple of weeks. Then I went out to see the family and spent a little time.

I talked with Marilyn quite regularly after Gary died. For a long time she went almost daily to the cemetery. She said she got great comfort just sitting and knowing he was there. She also told me that his mother was doing the same thing. It didn't surprise me too much that his mother was doing it, but I was rather surprised at how long it seemed to take Marilyn to say good-bye to Gary. Once, after Angie's wedding, Marilyn asked me if I would like to go to the cemetery at Camp Butler to see the tombstone. She had gotten a special tombstone and seemed to want me to see it. When we got there, Gary's mother and little Jennifer were waiting for us. It was one of the most elaborate tombstones I had ever seen. There was a lot of dirt, not much grass over Gary's plot. I asked Marilyn, "Have you decided not to plant grass, or did you plant it and it didn't grow, or what's happened?" "Oh, no, I don't want any grass on it, I like it this way, it really reminds me that Gary is there."

As a hospice home care volunteer, I followed the family for about one year after Gary died. I tried to help them get through Thanksgiving and, more especially, Christmas. Marilyn said, "I just don't have any heart to prepare for Christmas and don't care if we have a tree or not. Without Gary it won't be Christmas." After talking with her for some time, she did say she'd try to do something for the kids. I told her I'd like to help. One Saturday I invited a 13-year-old friend of mine to come with me to their home. She is a warm, loving girl and I knew she'd add a special something to this family. Marilyn had agreed to buy a little tree and we took along the trimmings and some snacks. Everyone seemed to enjoy the fun and fellowship in decorating the tree and we were able to say "Merry Christmas" with our hugs and tears. I felt Gary's presence when I looked up over the mantel and saw the family picture.

Esther's Story

Ready to Die

This is the story of the last three weeks of a woman's life and my role in walking the last journey with her and her son Rick. Esther died in 1980. The course of events enabled her to die in the way she requested, but this specific intervention was avant-garde 16 years ago. However, the same issues are current in today's medical world. Therefore, it is important to tell the story to help all of us in the decisions we need to make in our struggles surrounding dying and death.

Esther was a retired social worker who had put in 30 years of practice as a child welfare worker and psychiatric social worker. Rick was her only child for whom she had custody since a divorce when Rick was three years old. Mother/son bonding had begun early and was very deep until her death. Rick said, "Mother was the kind of person that people sought advice from, not only our family, but friends and co-workers as well."

Esther started smoking when she was in her late 20s and for many years smoked one to two packs a day. This caused many health problems, the most serious being emphysema, which resulted in her early retirement on disability. Shortly after retiring at the age of 57, Esther came to live with Rick, his wife Cindy and four children, ages three to nine. She only lived with them for about six months but, from the stories I heard from each of them, it was a very special time. As Esther had lived alone for many years and was very independent, she decided it best for all of them that she find her own place. She found a nice duplex across the street and lived there until she was no longer able to care for herself.

Following several hospitalizations over the next few years for respiratory problems, Esther's condition deteriorated until she was forced to remain in the hospital until her death. Attempts were made to wean her from the respirator. On two occasions she suffered a cardiac arrest. Each time she recovered, she expressed surprise that she was alive. She said, "I expected to die." When Rick asked her if she was afraid to die, she replied, "No." The second time she mouthed the word "Why" and kept repeating it. It seemed as though she thought that having a cardiac arrest was a good way to leave this world and was resentful she was revived.

She was again placed on the ventilator. Her physician stated that she had irreversible lung disease. On his next visit he noted that although she was mentally alert she also was very depressed by the turn of events. She asked her doctor to take her off the machine, saying she was ready to die. This is when I came into the picture.

I was asked by Esther's physician to visit her, because she had told him she was ready to die and wished to be taken off the respirator. This was not the first time she had expressed her wish not to be kept alive on the ventilator. Her only means of communication for several weeks was by writing on a tablet. She said she felt isolated from her family and the rest of the world. When I approached her bedside and introduced myself, I noticed the pad on which she wrote. She appeared quite calm and, after a few social comments, I decided it was important to discuss with Esther the primary reason for my visit to her. I said, "Esther, the nurses and your doctor tell me that you are ready to die and wish to come off the respirator. Is that true?" She nodded in affirmation and there was silence. I noticed a frown come on her brow and said, "Esther, is there something else that you would like to talk about, because I see you frowning." She nodded. I picked up the pad on which she had been communicating, and the first thing she wrote was "Funeral itself." She continued to write: "It would make it much easier for Rick if I came off the machine." At this point I asked her who Rick was, and she wrote, "My son."

I told Esther I would like to meet Rick. I asked her for his phone number, so I could make an appointment for him to come and talk about her wishes and where he was at in relation to all this. He sounded wary over the phone about coming to see me but did come in after work the following afternoon.

About 5 o'clock there was a knock on my door, and when I opened it there stood a handsome man, six feet tall, rather heavily set with red hair and a well-groomed red beard. After the initial conversation, Rick soon began to open up. And with that, he started to cry. He told me about the conversation between him and his mother the previous night. He said, "I told her I had an appointment to speak with you and as I did I just came apart. All of my plans to be strong and optimistic and positive had just fallen apart and I couldn't hold them together any longer. I wept and she put her arms around me and comforted me. I felt that I had really let her down. I was the one who was to be the strong one — she was the one who was dying. Everything had been turned around and when I fell apart her chances of recovering had fallen apart too."

Rick looked and sounded like a person in deep pain. I too felt sad as I listened to him begin to tell his story. But I believe a trusting relationship was begun during our first meeting that was important in helping him and his mother to achieve her wish. When he was finished and appeared less tearful, I said, "Think what a wonderful feeling your mother must have had to be able to comfort her son and give you this gift, a last gift." Rick replied, "I hadn't thought of it that way."

As we continued our conversation, I asked Rick about matters pertaining to what I call "unfinished business": the practical business of dying, of a will, insurance policies, funeral arrangements and other wishes. I asked him if he had talked to his mother about these matters. He replied, "No," and said, "They are exactly the opposite of what I want to talk about. Spring is coming and I want to talk about flowers and gardens and stuff and not about funerals." After a short silence, he went on to say, "Well, if she is going to die, would you please talk to her?"

I almost said I would — the great tendency for nurses to keep patients dependent on us — but I stopped myself short and said, "No, Rick, that is something I really believe needs to be done between you and your mother. I will help you in any way I can, but you really need to start it."

Rick replied, "I don't think I can do it, but I'll try."

The next morning I went to see Esther's doctor to tell him about the session I had with Rick. I said to him, "There are many issues at stake and many people involved. If we are going to help Esther have the kind of death she wishes and help Rick and his mother sort out some things, I believe we need to call a patient care conference." The doctor agreed to my request. It was not my responsibility to initiate this conference, and so I asked the doctor if he would discuss it with the nurse supervisor on Esther's nursing unit. I also tried to let him know how important it was for him to be present at the conference. He agreed. The following day, a patient care conference was held. Esther was told about the conference, but due to the severity of her illness it was not possible for her to be present. Also, although Rick was invited, he was unable to attend. I asked him if he had any special wishes and told him I would be an advocate for him. The chief nurse and doctor co-chaired the meeting. Present also were the social worker, a dietitian, because of Esther's likes and dislikes of food, and a priest. Although Esther had stated she didn't belong to a particular church, she indicated how important it was that a number of priests visited her, and Rick was an active Catholic. The priest's presence was also important because of the church's stand on the moral issues surrounding a request like Esther's to be taken off the respirator. Also present were the nurses on the unit who were caring for Esther and the respiratory therapist responsible for administering the treatment. Before proceeding with the conference, the nurse supervisor had consulted with the hospital administrator regarding the legal matters and obtained permission to proceed.

The doctor spoke first and said, "Esther's condition is irreversible and I agree with her wish to discontinue the respirator support as an extraordinary means for supporting life." The order was written, but no specific time was indicated. The conference allowed an opportunity for all present to talk about their own feelings about caring for Esther, and about participating in this unusual procedure of discontinuing life support or not. Everyone was permitted to make this choice. Esther and Rick were informed of these plans and seemed willing to work with the physician and staff.

Following the conference, I suggested that the staff not set a specific time for taking Esther off the respirator. It seemed that she and Rick needed as much time as they wished to do their business, enjoying time together saying good-byes, and doing some anticipatory grieving. They would tell us when they were ready. This plan was acceptable to all involved — Esther and Rick and the staff.

I met with Rick a few days later and he said, "I began to notice the same faces in mother's room when I would come in at night. People would read to her — mom liked to be read to from her *Newsweek* and columns from newspapers. These people developed a relationship with her and she developed a relationship with them. When I came in, the ones she liked especially, she would hold my hand and turn to them and say, 'This is my son, Rick.' "

The next time I saw Father Dick, he told me he had been asked whether or not Esther could join the Catholic Church. He said, "Rick was interested in this particularly. My concern was that Rick was trying to deal with Esther's death and whether he was asking his mother to become a Catholic in order to deal with her death. I wasn't convinced initially that that's really what Esther wanted. I didn't want to be forcing her into a church just because Rick was nervous about her dying. But as I got to know Esther, it became apparent that Esther wouldn't do anything unless she wanted to do it."

Once Rick was able to talk with his mom about her dying, he became more at ease. I sensed some letting go of the intense pain and tension that was present when I first met him. And because Esther continued to be mentally alert, they seemed to enjoy each other's company and shared a loving mother-son relationship. Rick's wife Cindy was also very loving and supportive. Together they told their four children of grandma's wishes to be taken off the respirator and her reasons. At first this was very difficult for the children to understand but, as they were able to visit Esther and see for themselves how difficult it was for her in her struggle to live, they became more accepting. Rick also told their relatives who lived within easy travelling distance. He explained the situation to them and they also came to visit Esther.

At the same time I was making the journey with Esther and Rick, I was also planning to visit my own mother in a nursing home in Calgary, Alberta. Her inability to walk due to severe arthritis in both knees had necessitated her moving into this home. She, like Esther, was mentally very alert. It was important for mom and me to have our time together. I was also there to help mom in this transition. Closing her home was a great loss for mom, my two brothers and myself. We no longer had a family home. In reflection, I believe it gave me a deeper understanding of the anticipatory grief that Rick and his mom must have been experiencing.

Once I noticed that Rick and his mom seemed to be more relaxed and the staff more accepting of Esther's wish to be taken off her ventilator, I made a reservation to fly to Calgary for a few days. Also there was no date set for discontinuing her treatment. I informed them and her doctor of my plans and left. Although I had no confirmation that Esther would still be alive when I returned, I needed to trust myself that this decision was correct. Mother and I had a good visit and I felt at ease in leaving her in a few days. She seemed peaceful in her new home, owned by the Lutheran Church. She had belonged to the Lutheran Church when she was growing up and was delighted to have returned to her religious roots.

When I returned to Springfield I was somewhat surprised to find Esther still living with little change and still very alert mentally. Rick seemed very pleased to have me back. Within a few days he told the doctor that he and his mom were ready to have her come off the respirator, to "pull the plug." They set the date and time: Tuesday morning at 10 o'clock, exactly three weeks from the day we held the family conference.

Rick vividly recalled this period of finally letting go of his mom. "On Monday night I asked mom what she wanted for supper and she said pizza — pizza and wine." Cindy and I joined her for supper and it was a good pizza. We all enjoyed it. She knew, of course, that she was going off the respirator the next day. She had requested to become a Catholic, to die a Catholic and have a funeral mass. I thought, how symbolic of the Last Supper!

Tuesday morning Esther was baptized and took communion. Rick and Father Dick were with her, also her doctor, her special nurses and the respiratory therapist. I was there to try to lend moral support. It was an intensely emotional time for all of us. Her doctor had explained to her what would happen to her once she came off the ventilator: she'd be a little more short of breath. As soon as she was taken off the ventilator, she became very apprehensive, which increased her difficulty in breathing. The respiratory therapist gave her some oxygen through a mask, but it did little to relieve her extreme discomfort. Although her doctor had also prescribed a small dose of a sedative, he soon had to prescribe a more potent drug. In telling his story, he said, "Esther was in a lot of discomfort as a result of this discontinuation of the respirator and I made a decision, for the sake of giving her some comfort and tranquilization, to use Valium despite the fact that I knew it was going to suppress her respiration somewhat." It worked rather well. She became calm while still conscious and then slowly became comatose and lost consciousness.

Rick never left her side. Cindy was there supporting him, as were the nurses. I remained nearby until early evening, when I went home. I knew that Esther was at peace in her dying and all was well.

I was back on the ward early the next morning. Rick and Cindy had remained at Esther's bedside all night. In the morning, although her respirations were becoming slower, Rick had decided to run home, say hello to their children and take a shower. Shortly after he left, the nurses turned Esther on her side to rub her back and make her more comfortable. While doing this, Esther stopped breathing. One of the nurses, speaking into Esther's ear said, "Esther, you can't die yet. Rick isn't here." Another nurse phoned him to come quickly and Esther began to breathe again. She was turned onto her back and within a short time Rick arrived. As I was coming down the hall towards Esther's room, I met Rick frantically running in the same direction. He went directly to his mother's side and, holding her in his arms, she peacefully stopped breathing. I vividly remember standing behind him, one hand on his shoulder, supporting him as best I could. A hush came over the room. Esther was dead. No one was in a hurry to leave the room as we all needed time to say good-bye to this beautiful and courageous woman we had come to love dearly. And so we were able to comfort each other with our hugs and our tears.

I spent time with Rick and Cindy before they left for home to tell their four children. They were not sure whether to bring the children to the funeral, but allowing them some time to begin their own grief work, they were able to discuss it. They came to their own conclusion to bring the children. I went to the funeral with some of the staff from Esther's ward. The first thing I noticed when we entered the sanctuary was a group of school children sitting in the balcony. They were classmates of Esther's oldest grandchild and they sang a hymn during the service. Rick and Cindy approached me and invited me to go forward with them to see Esther lying in the open coffin. They pointed out to us the four red tulips lying beside her. Each one of her grandchildren picked a fresh tulip from Esther's garden and laid it beside her. What courage and what beauty!

Father Dick delivered the homily. This is what he told friends after the service. "The homily that I was able to preach was not a review of Esther's life but rather the review of her dying. I tried to sum up that the miracle was not just in the way she lived but in the whole way in which she was enabled to die. The depth of humanness that was possible for her in death was the real meaning in any kind of religious funeral service that could be celebrated to sum up her life and say a final farewell to her."

I visited the family shortly after the funeral to help them with their grieving. They invited me to eat with them on several occasions and we always enjoyed that time together. It allowed time for them to talk about Esther and tell stories of their relationships over the years. It also gave me the opportunity to get to know parts of Esther's life before her illness. Walking the journey with such a remarkable family was truly a gift.

Esther's story is a contemporary example of how we, the caregivers, may share in the life and the death of a patient who requested to have her life support — a ventilator — discontinued. It vividly describes how the patient, her family and the health care team were enabled to resolve some of their own conflicting feelings that surround death.

Ann's Story

*Floy,
Ann's mother,
in her younger years.*

*Alzheimer's —
The Long Good-bye*

This story tells how death peacefully released Ann and her mother Floy from 14 years of turmoil, pain and suffering. Floy was a victim of that dreaded, debilitating disease of today — Alzheimer's. This story is important because of the impact of this extended, hopeless disease on patient, family and society and its many unique facets associated with loss and grief. It reveals some of the problems associated with the gradual decline of a loved mother inflicted with dementia, and the effects on her daughter and others in the family. As Ann's friend over the years, my role became one of attentive listener, comforter, supporter and, at times, mentor, especially during the final three years of Floy's life.

Family history and relationships play a significant part in the care and support of the patient and the primary caregiver. Ann was blessed by being born into a family that gave her the emotional and spiritual resources she needed to enable her to walk the long, painful journey with her mother. At one point she reflected, "We're a strong family that has allegedly nurtured each other all along the way. We grew up with two parents who were incredibly nurturing folk and shared their issues as a family council." The nurturing, openness and truthtelling were adopted by Ann as the model for the family life she shared with her husband Pete and their two sons. As an outsider I admired this, as well as the space and privacy they gave each other. Ann's work did not allow much time for social gatherings. Thus our early relationship began with noon luncheons usually arranged by her minister. It took a little time to feel at ease with this well-groomed, self-assured, energetic lady who appeared to need the spotlight in any conversation. However, I soon became aware of another side of Ann. As we talked about spiritual issues, I recognized a person very committed to her church and her faith.

Ann could be described as a workaholic. She often worked 16 to 18-hour days and yet found time to be involved with church activities. I also observed her, on more than one occasion, walking with a fellow traveller in need. When her minister was diagnosed with multiple sclerosis, Ann was faithfully there when he needed her. She was also a great organizer and able to admit her own limitations by asking others to help. Her prayer life was important to her. She said, "The Lord and I spend a lot of time together. We deal with our issues, and the Spirit and I are pretty much in touch on that."

In knowing Ann and listening to her describe her mom, it seems these two women had much in common. "My mother was the kind of a woman who always thought she could be there for everyone. She didn't get sick. She was a role model for me, a feminist before there were feminists, and was just a part of me." Talking about her mom shortly after she died, Ann also said, "It's interesting how passionately I cared for my mom."

In 1974 Pete's father Bill died following a long battle with lung cancer. Although Pete had been with his father at the time of surgery, seven years before, and visited on a few other occasions, Pete's mother had not kept him abreast of the seriousness of his father's illness. He was hospitalized shortly before he died, alone. Pete's mother phoned to give him the sad news, but he was out of town. Ann took the call and was left with the responsibility of telling Pete.

Also in 1974, Ann's father retired. Prior to his retirement, Ann's mother was seemingly a very healthy person. During the next three years the family noticed some gradual changes in Floy's mental ability, but Ann's father protected her and made all the decisions. It was only following his sudden death in 1977 from a heart attack that Floy's family was presented with the dilemma regarding their mother's mental status: was this normal depression following the sudden death of a husband, and/or dementia?

Ann had two siblings but was the only one living in the same state as her parents, so much of the caregiving responsibility fell on her shoulders. She had a younger sister Gretchen living in Japan in 1974, and a brother Rick living in California. When asked how her sister and brother dealt with the multiple changes in their mother's behavior, she replied, "At first they dealt with it by not being a part of it. My brother did his level best from a distance to deal with it. He came in regularly, checking on mom and on me. He was phenomenally good on checking on me. My sister basically never has dealt with it."

When asked what this did to their relationship, she replied, "We've had to work harder on it. She is seven and a half years younger than I am and always looked up to me as the older sister for whatever reason. I've been on a pedestal that I didn't know I had. We've been working on that. I've always loved my sister and she's always loved me. That's never been the issue, but we're products of two different generations. I came out of the 1950s and 1960s, but she is totally a 1960s product. We've dealt with issues differently, including our mother. She dealt with mother in her own way. It never enabled her to spend much of her time with mom."

Ann, her sister and brother jointly decided to make arrangements for their mother to remain in her own apartment in the Chicago area. They consulted Floy's doctor for advice, and he told them the facts regarding their mother's illness and what to expect. Arrangements were made for necessary assistance which would support her but allow her some independence too. Eventually the slow deterioration that takes place with Alzheimer's necessitated some drastic changes. When Floy was no longer able to manage her own affairs, the three children were forced to intercede. She had lost the ability to care for herself and her home. Ann describes visiting her apartment: "There was nothing on the cupboards, every dish in the whole house was in the sink or on the counter, her bathroom was unkempt, just a plethora of signs that we had to move in massively." Ann obtained power of attorney, and they made arrangements to move Floy into a Presbyterian home in Springfield (where Ann and her family lived). Ann describes that move as the beginning of a battle that continued until her mother died seven years later.

There were many losses that occurred as a result of the decision to move Floy to Springfield. The loss of independence and self-esteem for a lady who had at one time been a role model for her daughter, a professional and a homemaker must have been very difficult.

Floy's ability to reason and make choices was also lost. When Ann moved her into the Presbyterian home, Floy got very angry. She wanted her own apartment and proclaimed, "I'm going to cook again," though she hadn't cooked in two years. Perhaps the greatest loss was her car. Here the battle really raged over the question of her driver's license. It was very difficult for Ann to make the decision to take away her mother's car, but she felt she had no other choice. Temporarily her mother's only recourse was to fight back. Anger is one of the strongest emotions. The book *The 36-Hour Day* is helpful in trying to understand how a person with a progressively dementing illness overreacts and experiences rapidly changing moods.

These behavioral changes are very difficult for the caregiver to understand, especially in the earlier stages of the disease. Ann — an intelligent, well-educated, sensitive and committed Christian — was no exception. She expressed some of her own frustrations, helplessness, anger and wanting to run away. "Mother rose up and said incredibly dreadful things. She accused me of taking her money, abusing her. There were times when my anger was more intense than I've ever known it." At first Ann chose to deal with her anger through tears but admitted that mostly she did not deal with it except inside herself. As her mother's disease progressed, Ann began to change her own behavior. She said, "I started to deal with each one of my issues, telling myself that my life, my sanity are more important than whatever else happens." At this juncture she also became interested in the Alzheimer's support group.

I was privileged to be a board member of our local Alzheimer's association chapter and also chairperson of the Alzheimer's family support group at that time. In the beginning of my responsibilities there, it was important to learn as much as I could about the disease itself, the educational material available and the research being carried out. However, my real learning occurred when I became involved with the family members in the support group. To listen to their stories every month and to find ways to help them cope day-by-day was a new challenge for me. I remember several men in particular who shared and exchanged recipes with each other and with me. I really looked forward to our meetings and to our sharing with laughter, tears and sometimes despair. And for Ann the group was truly a blessing. She said, "Unless I got involved with the support group, I knew I was going to be the victim — I was going to be the sick person while mother didn't even know what was going on. When I began to talk and did not keep it inside myself, it enabled me to go forward. I tried to learn everything I could. *The 36-Hour Day* was one of the first books I bought."

As Floy's dementia slowly worsened, it became necessary to move her into a nursing home with a special unit for Alzheimer's patients. Here she lived the last three years of her life. Many family members have a difficult time visiting their loved one in this state of degeneration. This family was no exception. Ann told me, "No one except me could regularly go in, week after week, and look at her."

This also was a very difficult time for Floy's two grandsons, Bob and David. When they were very young — especially Bob, the older son — they spent considerable time with their grandparents. Bob had a very difficult time dealing with his grandfather's sudden death in 1977 and then the slow torturous death of his grandmother. Bob and David were at college by the time Floy was moved to the nursing home, but when home on weekends they seldom went to visit their grandmother. Bob chose to deal with his grief by writing a term paper on dementia. Rather than taking a coldly academic approach, Bob phoned and interviewed all his immediate relatives in his attempt to understand Alzheimer's.

Ann was very faithful in visiting her mother on a regular basis. From time to time she would share with me how very difficult it was to visit when her mother didn't even know her. In the summer of 1986, Ann decided she needed some respite care, and so she and David went to Europe for three weeks. When Ann returned, she was shocked to see how thin and listless Floy had become. Ann had told her mother her travel plans for days before she left for the trip, and the staff at the nursing home had reminded Floy daily. But the staff noticed that the decline in her appetite, weight and spirit began at this time and continued until her death.

About a week before Floy died, Ann phoned me and asked if there was anything special she needed to have done to make certain that no extraordinary measures would be carried out in her mother's final days. I recommended that she check with the nursing staff to see that her doctor's orders complied with that wish. She also asked if there would be any marked changes in her mother as death approached. My own mother had died four years before, one month after a stroke. She had requested an order be written for "no extra ordinary measures" before her stroke, which included no forcing of fluids. I was with mother to help her in her dying and was able to share this with Ann. This seemed helpful for her at this difficult time.

One morning Ann phoned to tell me that she and Pete were out at the nursing home. They had received a phone call telling them her mother's respirations had become very difficult, her color poor and the staff did not think she would live another 24 hours. It was suggested that Ann call her sister in Florida and her brother in California. While we were on the phone, Ann said, "I've never seen anybody die. What will it be like?" I asked if she wanted me to come out, and she said, "No, Pete's here with me and we're just quietly sitting with mom."

Part of me heard what Ann said, but my heart and my feelings were telling me to go out and just be present. When I arrived Ann was at her mother's bedside. I had never met Floy, so Ann introduced me to her. There was no apparent response. Although her respirations were shallow, she didn't seem to be in any great distress. Ann remarked on the high quality of nursing care her mother had received, and this was obvious from what I observed. Ann said, "My sister will be in about 5:30 and my brother about 10:30. My greatest wish is that mom will be alive until they arrive." I suggested that she talk directly into her mom's ear and tell her that. She had been doing this already, but I said it might be important to reinforce the message frequently.

Ann suggested we go out into the lounge for awhile. I noticed Pete standing there, slumped over and crying. He joined us and, with tears in his eyes, began to talk about his father who had been dead for 14 years. He talked about how terrible it had been for him because his mother had not called him ahead of time to allow him to get there and see his dad before he died. He said, "I feel I have been cheated. I never had a chance to say good-bye to my dad and I still have a lot of anger towards my mother. I hope Bob and Gretchen will be able to get here so they can say good-bye to their mother, so they won't have these feelings that I'm still dealing with."

Ann did a lot of crying that afternoon too. She and Pete were able to hold each other and cry together. And so, after 14 years, Pete was able to begin his grieving for the death of his father. I believe this was truly a spiritual experience for each of us. While Ann was grieving the anticipated death of her mother, Pete was freed to feel and begin his delayed grief for his father. I saw myself as a friend, a believer and an enabler. Each of us was a gift to each other.

I sat with Ann and Pete for about two hours. Periodically, Ann or I would go in and give her mom a hug and talk to her but didn't stay in Floy's room. Pete chose to remain in the lounge. They appeared fairly calm, so I left. Shortly after Gretchen arrived, I phoned Ann that evening just to say "Hi" and asked her to call me if she needed me. I phoned the nursing home the next morning and the nurse told me that Floy had died about 2:00 a.m. Ann phoned later and sounded almost exuberant over the phone. She said, "Bob arrived about 10:30 p.m. We all stayed for a short time and then left so Bob would have his time alone with mom."

Bob told them he was able to talk with his mom and he believed that at times she was aware he was there. He had called them at 1:30 to tell them their mom was sinking into a deeper coma. Ann continued, "We all got out there in time. With all of us together, mother died in our arms. It was so beautiful; it was so peaceful and we were all there. It's almost as though we lived a whole lifetime with our mother in those last few hours." Later she told me that Pete had said how helpful it had been for him to have his time in the afternoon to begin grieving for his father, which had enabled him to support Ann, Rick and Gretchen as they began their grief work.

Some families honor a loved one who has just died with a celebration. That was a beautiful experience for this family. Ann shared the event with me. "The catharsis due to mother's death was incredible. Because all of us dealt with some issues as we watched her die, we were ready to celebrate when we went back to our house. At 5:00 a.m. we all toasted with a glass of whatever we had in our hand to whatever our issues were. It was the most healing moment I knew in our family. It was like telling mom that in her death she enabled issues in people's lives to come forward. It was really beautiful. I would wish for every family the opportunity to see the healing that death brings, the closure. Just an extremely spiritual time."

The family had agreed that an autopsy be performed following Floy's death and that she be cremated. Thus there was no visitation. And because Floy had moved to live near Ann and Pete due to her condition, she really had no local friends — thus no memorial service at this time. I suggested to Ann that her mother's friends at the nursing home who had cared for her the last three years of her life needed their time to grieve and say good-bye. Ann went out and spent time with them.

In about two weeks, Ann and Pete left for Florida to visit his mother. Ann described the intensity of her own grief there. She said, "I can remember crying for almost 24 hours and saying to Peter, 'I don't think anyone loves me any more. My parents are gone and no one will love me ever again.'" They were walking on the beach and she said, "Here he was hugging me and holding me and I'm not feeling any love. It just got crazy. It only lasted 24 hours, thank God. In that 24-hour period, that man did everything that he could possibly do. But I had to walk that journey. I had to let my parents go." She also said, "I'm not sure he could have done that for me if you hadn't helped him to finally deal with his dad."

A memorial service for Floy was held in June back in her hometown near Chicago. Ann described this as the true funeral, a time for really saying good-bye. It was especially meaningful for the two grandsons, Bob and David. Bob hadn't shed a tear when he was told his grandmother had died. David had cried a lot. The day of the funeral David was able to get through the service with composure, and Bob was the one who had some difficulty. He had asked to participate in the service, but when he stood up to talk about his grandmother, he just couldn't and sat down. After a brief time he stood up again and was able to say what he had in his heart. He told all of those present what a wonderful woman she was and how badly he felt that he walked away from her when she was a patient in the nursing home. The memorial service was an opportunity for the family to come together, to do more grief work, to honor their mother and grandmother, to celebrate her life and say a final farewell to a special lady.

Alzheimer's can be called the long good-bye. You grieve about the loved one from the moment you begin to observe the gradual loss of memory and the speech and personality changes, because they are incurable. The person you love is gradually changing before your eyes. You say good-bye many times until the final good-bye at death. For Ann and her family, the journey was extremely long — 14 years. Although Ann was fearful that she might become the victim, through her own prayer and understanding of self-worth she chose a positive path. She became a member of the Alzheimer's family support group. Storytelling is the central theme for these groups. They allow participants to discover they are not alone but are with other persons who are also struggling with saying the long good-bye to their loved ones, and who understand and empathize. This sharing often gives strength and peace of mind. For Ann it was very helpful and also allowed her to share her gifts of herself. In the end, she and her family were enabled to do the grief work they needed to do before saying their final good-bye to Floy.

Norma's Story

Part II

Growth through Loss

*Norma with Terry Mast, left, and Jay Kennerly
around the table in Norma's home where they have been
meeting every week, for eight years.*

My commitment to write this book, with my two fellow travellers Terry and Jay, has inspired me to do a life review. It has been a spiritual journey, reliving many parts of my life to date. "Norma's Story, Part I: The Gift of Tears" identified some of my key shaping experiences related to dying and death. After I left home to begin my nursing career, the course of my life was anything but static. Work, travel and educational opportunities have taken me to many places. Each move was exciting but also meant a loss of friends, familiar surroundings, pulling up roots I'd planted, saying good-byes and beginning again. It was not always easy, especially establishing new relationships. And so I frequently experienced loneliness and a desire to be loved. However, I also found each new job a challenge which demanded much of me, and so I forged ahead. I did not discover for many years that there can be growth through our losses and changes.

Now, in reflection, I realize I had been learning while living many of life's experiences. And thus at the age of 60, when many persons are making plans to retire, I began a new journey in what was, for me, a new country: the United States of America.

It was July 1978 when I accepted a faculty position in the Department of Medical Humanities and Surgery at the Southern Illinois University (SIU), School of Medicine in Springfield, Illinois. This new venture for me really began a year earlier, in mid-1977, at a workshop on the "Care of the Terminally Ill" at St. Francis Xavier University in Antigonish, Nova Scotia. The leader of the workshop, a pioneer in the field of dying and death, was Dr. Glen Davidson, Chairman of the Department of Medical Humanities in Springfield. Little did I realize then that one year later I would be invited to join his department at SIU. I had been invited to present a paper at the workshop describing the nursing model for hospice we had developed at the Victoria General Hospital in Halifax. Dr. Davidson was impressed with the model we had developed and, following the workshop, he invited me to write a chapter for a book he was editing, *The Hospice: Development and Administration*. This was the first attempt to bring together a report on the hospice movement in North America in one volume. At the same time I discussed with Dr. Davidson my desire to further my knowledge in this specialized area.

Glen invited me to be a "fellow" in his department for a month. Thus I applied for a study leave and was off to Springfield in the spring of 1978. It seems ironic now that I arrived there on Easter Monday, when the city was recovering from a severe ice storm. I became very involved with teaching, church and good friends, yet I was anxious to return to Halifax, a beautiful city in the country where I believed I was going to be.

Dr. Davidson drove me to the airport in Springfield. I was more than grateful to him for making it possible for me to have such a rich learning experience and to meet and share with fellow nurses and professionals and to hear about the unique Medical Humanities faculty and their slow integration of a new program into the curriculum. Naturally he asked me for my opinions. Among other comments, I said, "I think you have a fine department, but when are you going to get a nurse aboard?" It was then time to board my plane and say a final farewell. So I thought. A phone call a month later resulted in an invitation to return for interviews for a possible faculty appointment. And subsequently I officially crossed the border in October 1978 with a green card headed "Resident Alien."

The move to Springfield was another leap in faith. I had learned, through the changes and accompanying losses over the years, some of the "how to's." And I believe there are many advantages to aging. I take more risks and try to live one day at a time. I also can claim a lifetime of experiences in living with and caring for the dying. None of this did I have when I first cared for dying Johnny as a young student nurse. Now to become a professor in the Department of Medical Humanities under the chairmanship of Dr. Glen Davidson was another dream come true. For many years I had believed there was a special role for a nurse, as a full faculty member, to teach medical students. It took many years for me to be heard and, in fact, I had to leave my own country before this became a reality. I'm grateful for my strong Scottish-German heritage — never give up if you really believe in something.

A department of medical humanities within a medical school was unusual in 1978. Dr. Davidson's was one of the first. But changes were taking place in medical education. Purely physician faculties were beginning to shift to inter-disciplinary teams of professionals teaching in collegial relationships. SIU, being a new medical school, had many advantages. One important one was that the dean was a man of great vision and had carefully selected key players who were capable of new discoveries. I was a bit frightened but over-joyed to be a member of this team. I had requested a cross-appointment in a clinical department — my real laboratory. SIU's chairman of surgery made this possible. I was aware of breaking new ground as a nurse and a full professor in a highly specialized area. And I was teaching a non-scientific subject: psycho-social care. But I believed strongly in the wholistic approach to care, had a strong clinical background and a feeling of self-worth and belief in myself. It was not easy at first. My abilities coupled with the strong support I received from the chairman of the surgery department, Dr. J. Roland Folse, my greatest advocate, not only allowed me to survive but to grow with the pain and the joy in this new venture.

My cross-appointment in the Departments of Medical Humanities and Surgery made me the first nurse in North America to be given a full professorship with tenure in a medical school and was paramount to my belief in integrating theory and practice. Thus it was essential for me to have a clinical appointment. This had a two-fold effect: it allowed me to have direct input into the curriculum and teaching of the surgical clerkship, including student evaluations, and it allowed me to continue as a clinician "on the wards." I received consultations from the faculty in the department and did counseling with the patients and their families referred to me. One of the chapters in this book, "Esther's Story," illustrates well how I worked directly with doctors and staff. It was the team functioning optimally to provide total care. Most of the patients for whom I was asked to consult were diagnosed with a terminal illness, which again made me grateful for my time spent at St. Christopher's Hospice in 1974, which had truly given me the confidence to use my skills in this highly specialized area.

My major teaching responsibilities were to teach students psycho-social skills in the clinical setting. This was not easy, especially in a specialty such as surgery, with all the high technology of today. With much emphasis still on cure, to discuss care and the use of self was somewhat in discord with conventional medical practice. This was especially true in relating to dying and death.

The Department of Medical Humanities developed a special, optional one-week program for third-year students. General topics were offered by the faculty from which students could choose two. I offered one called "The Physician and the Terminally Ill Patient." Only a few students chose it, but those who did reported it to be a very rich experience. I hope every medical school will soon make such a course mandatory. Mine is described in some detail in my book, *The Role of the Nurse in Clinical Medical Education.*

St. John's Hospital, one of the large hospitals affiliated with SIU's medical school, was one of my major clinical areas. It also had begun plans for the development of a hospice, and Dr. Davidson was a member of the hospital's planning committee. As such, he committed his department to support and provide assistance, as requested, in all phases of development of the hospice, to be the first in Illinois. Part of my original contract was to be a part-time consultant to the planning committee as long as my services were needed. This hospice development work provided me with an opportunity to continue the work I had begun in Halifax. I was beginning to see the many threads in my life becoming woven together like a beautiful tapestry.

When I joined the planning committee, one of the key figures, the medical director, had not yet been appointed. The hospice philosophy, as created by Dr. Cecily Saunders, was new to most physicians in the States, and most medical schools did not include care of the terminally ill in their curriculum. Thus, pain and symptom control and open communication related to dying and death needed to be taught to many, professionals and public alike. It was a gigantic task, but St. John's Hospice found the right doctor — Dr. Robert Nachtway, an internist with a human approach to his patients, colleagues, staff and families, and a man of deep faith. Dr. Nachtway also had an openness and willingness to learn new approaches to care for the terminally ill — an answer to our prayers. The planning demanded a lot of hard work. Through long tedious meetings — but with commitment, team spirit and a sense of humor — the St. John's Hospice came into being, with an in-patient unit, a home care program and plans for a bereavement program. With much celebration, the first home care patient was admitted on February 1, 1980. My major commitment as a consultant concluded, although I continued to assist in the training programs for new staff members and volunteers. At this writing I am still a hospice home care volunteer, and my life continues to be enriched in walking this journey with patients and their families.

At the age of 85, my mother became a patient at Bethany Auxiliary Hospital in Calgary, Alberta, while I was assisting the St. John's Hospice to develop. Bethany was begun by the Lutheran Church and had a strong religious affiliation, as demonstrated in many ways. The Pastoral Care Department played a major role with its leadership and program. As my mother had grown up in a Lutheran Church in Kitchener, Ontario, it was like coming home for her. She wasn't there long before she had developed a deep friendship with the senior pastor, known as Pastor Del. I visited mom as often as I could, and pastor Del and I became good friends. I told him all about our hospice program at St. John's and we discussed the possibility of developing a unit within Bethany. I offered to do a one-day workshop, if he and his staff were interested. The result was that in October 1980 — when I was there for mom's birthday — it took place. And who do you think took a seat in the front row? Yes, my mom. I was so proud to have her there. In her own quiet way, mom became a caregiver. She would hand-drive her wheelchair to visit some of the patients, and on at least one occasion went to sit with a dying patient. She never told me about the special visits, but pastor Del gave me a picture of my mother ministering. When she died on July 28, 1984, my two brothers and I gave a donation to assist in the establishment of the hospice program at Bethany Auxiliary Hospital — one of the first in Canada in a nursing home.

As the hospice movement began to grow across North America, support groups were rapidly being formed. Sister Margaret, one of the nuns in the pastoral care department at St. John's Hospital, recognized the needs of widows after the loss of a spouse, made plans to form a support group and invited me to help her. Only a few women were present for our first meeting in mid-1979. For some, it was the first time anyone had listened to their story. And stories they told!

I remember one woman who told about the sudden death of her husband, a school teacher. They were in their car on their way to a school ball game when they were hit by a drunken driver. Kay's husband was fatally injured instantly, fell over and died in her lap. Although she received some injuries, she was rescued. But she had 12 children, ages seven to 23, waiting for her at home. Kay was in deep shock, numbness and pain, and suffered greatly for months after her husband died. She told me she just wanted to run away and,

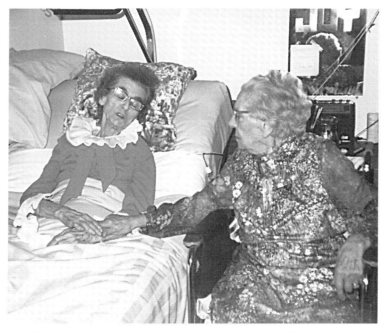

Mother ministering to another patient at Bethany Auxiliary Hospital.

in a sense, she did. Within nine months she had made three major moves. Daily she prayed, "Please God, let me die." Just to look at her one could recognize a woman in deep pain. Fortunately, her children were a great blessing. They were all good students, and two of the older ones "mothered" the little ones until Kay began to recover. She received much support from the then-small widows group and also came to me for private counseling. I admired her courage, deep faith and spirit for survival and believe I helped in her healing, but she did much of the grief work herself until she was free to fully live again.

Several years later, when Sister Margaret moved away, this

same Kay became the group leader. I remember being a guest when the group had grown to 60 or 70, with a number of widowers there also. I was so excited to see her in front of the group. As she directed the members into smaller groups, I heard her saying, "Maybe we should tell some of our stories today and make them funny stories. We need to get some humor in this place." And they did. It was a privilege for me to have watched the growth of this support group and the healing that occurred because of it. I believe grief work is hard work — physically, emotionally and spiritually — and cannot easily be done alone.

Many seminars and workshops related to loss and terminal illnesses have emerged across the country for professionals, caregivers and fellow travellers. I have received a number of invitations from groups within Springfield and beyond. In 1983, I made my first visit to Dallas, Texas. I almost thought I was back to my roots in Alberta, with the ten-gallon hats, cowboy boots and cattle. I had been invited to be the guest speaker at a two-day workshop called "Helping the Caregiver Cope with Grief." It was presented by the Department of Nursing at the Baylor University Medical Center, but the program planning committee was multidisciplinary. I received a warm welcome from my western friends. It was good to share our concerns related to such a human topic.

A year later I was back in Dallas, this time to interview the late Norman Cousins for a videotape I was authoring on "The Artistry of Medicine" to use in teaching psycho-social care to medical students. I had often quoted him in my classes and workshops with special reference to his communication skills. He stated that good communication is the lifeline to survival.

His recovery from his supposedly incurable illness prompted him to write the classic book, *Anatomy of an Illness as Perceived by the Patient*. He believed that negative emotions produced negative chemistry and reasoned that "love, hope, faith, laughter, confidence and the will to live have therapeutic value." It was a privilege to meet him. An informal breakfast together gave me time to reduce my stress before the actual interview began, although I had done my homework and was as prepared as one can be. This videotape and his books became valuable additions to our library.

About that time, the hospice program at the Victoria General Hospital in Halifax planned two two-day workshops on "Care of the Terminally Ill" and invited me to assist with the teaching. I had no hesitation in accepting. I had been gone for four years and was anxious to return for personal as well as professional reasons. I felt I had left a piece of me there and perhaps it needed a little nourishing. We had a wonderful time with very receptive participants. I vividly remember doing some role playing with the medical director of the hospice, a psychiatrist dearly beloved by everyone. There was a spirit conducive to learning. One of our first hospice volunteers, who was terminally ill with cancer, was also present. Her bouncy and positive attitude was rich and meaningful. Lots of joy and laughter and sadness and tears were experienced. We enjoyed having lunch together and did some reminiscing about the early beginnings of the Victoria General Hospice. She died shortly after I returned to Springfield.

I have discovered while teaching medical students about the psycho-social needs of terminally ill patients and their families that there are many losses other than death itself, which is the final loss. Many patients referred to me were cancer patients in the terminal phase of their illness. We tell a few of their stories in this book. However, many were more recently diagnosed and their needs were different. They were just beginning a journey often laden with fear, anger, denial and social isolation. Nan's story describes some of these feelings and emotions during the early stages of her illness.

Similar emotions were present among patients suffering from severe trauma. I remember a young father whose face was badly burned in a fire. He had a wife and two young children. The children longed to see their father again, but he, his wife and some of the staff were fearful of the children's reactions. It was Christmastime and each had made a special gift for their dad. I suggested we have a photo taken of him; first we would tell the children as much as we could and then we would gradually show them his picture. To everyone's surprise, they did not turn away. Instead, they really wanted to see him. Fortunately, he could hear and so they were able to tell him they loved him, give him his gifts and just be present with him and their mom. There weren't many dry eyes among those of us nearby. What a glorious Christmas gift for all involved, especially the family.

Once again I was aware of the importance of teaching wholistic health and illness, body/mind and spirit. I developed a framework which illustrated the whole process from birth to death: Living/Aging/Dying/Grieving/Death. Each is a part of the whole and intertwines as one life cycle.

Through walking the journey with many people, I have observed that some are able to tolerate more pain — physically, emotionally and spiritually — than others. Although I believe I am a compassionate person and am able to cry or laugh or listen as needed, I cannot feel what each person feels.

John McFarland, who wrote *Now That I Have Cancer I Am Whole*, describes this well from his own experiences. He writes, "Feeling is spiritual, it digs deep into the heart of truth that cannot be spoken but only experienced. During the time of our pain, we actually become more real as persons because we are more individual, spiritual, unique."

Robert Pope, in his profound book, *Illness and Healing: Images of Cancer* gave hope to those of us inflicted with a terminal or life-threatening illness when he wrote, "Humans have a great capacity to adapt and to grow. In this ability rests our future in dealing with cancer and, indeed, all of life." And thus from my own framework and continuous teaching, caring and searching, there has evolved a model I call "Growth Through Loss." My friend Kay, whom you met earlier in this chapter, powerfully exemplifies growth through loss.

Aging, one of the phases in our life cycle, has its own special needs. Many losses occur along with the gains. And so I have developed a program focusing on "Growth Through Loss" that can be adapted to all age groups. I have conducted a number of weekend workshops in local churches, working closely with ministers and planning committees. I remember a father and daughter being present, their losses being his wife and her mother through divorce. The father was a recovering alcoholic. He and his daughter were having a difficult time communicating. Many tears were shed during the weekend, but these two were supported by the group with hugs, listening ears and love. Their reunion at our closing worship service, with everyone holding hands in a circle, was a small miracle for them. I do believe there is healing power in touch, in a hug. Robert Pope's painting "Hug" symbolizes this for me. Robert said, "The gesture of the hug is life-affirming."

In 1989 I was invited back to Canada to participate in a palliative care conference held in Shediac, New Brunswick, sponsored by the New Brunswick Extra-Mural Hospital and Hospice in Shediac. And so after 11 years I was returning to my Maritime roots again. What joy and excitement! I suggested to the planning committee that they may wish to subtitle the conference "Growth Through Loss," which they did. About 200 health professionals and volunteers from the three Maritime provinces came for two full days. The auditorium was alive with readiness to learn, share and have some fun. A gala event got us off to a fine start at 8 a.m. on Monday morning; it was Blaine, a volunteer, who happened to be blind, playing the bagpipes. I'll never forget that, nor, I'm sure, will anyone else who was there. Later in the program, Blaine gave a fine presentation on the place of music therapy in the healing process. It was a remarkable two days with much to learn from each other and share with each other. A glorious feed of lobsters in the evening gave us renewed energy and play time. The conference closed with the theme "Journey from Brokenness to Wholeness." Again, Blaine led us in a celebration with his bagpipes, while we sang "Life is flowing like a river" and then enjoyed a special birthday cake to celebrate life. There were many tears when it came time to say good-bye to new friends. Blaine died some time later with complications from diabetes. He was blessed with a beautiful wife who, with the help of hospice volunteers, cared for him at home until death took over. He will long be remembered for giving all he had. Thank you, Blaine.

Two of the major losses that changed the course of my life happened in the mid-1980s: my mother's death and my retirement. July 28, 1984, is a day I'll never forget. My own dear mother died in Bethany Auxiliary Hospital at the age of almost 90. She had lived a full, rich life and had indeed made a very positive adjustment to living her last four and a half years in an institution. When I was with her for our last Christmas together she talked with me about an order being placed on her chart that "no extra ordinary" measures be carried out should she have a stroke or any other mishap. We also met with her pastor and she planned her funeral. I was so proud of her for taking the initiative, but that was true to her character — a great planner and always so thoughtful of others. I informed my two brothers of her wishes. And so she took care of all her unfinished business before she had a stroke at the end of June that left her unable to talk.

When I received a phone call from my younger brother informing me that our mother was critically ill, I left immediately for Calgary. Calgary seemed so far away and I feared she might die before I could get there. Mom had never been sick, and so it was difficult to see her so ill with a very high temperature. The stroke had affected the part of her brain that controls body temperature. I immediately rolled up my nursing sleeves and helped care for her. She was able to recognize me but unable to talk, except occasionally I heard her say "Norma." I became her primary caregiver. Some of the staff tried to force her to drink, and so I had some teaching to do also. I spent many hours just sitting beside her, holding her hand, talking to her and just being together.

It was not easy to watch my mother slowly die. But I was blessed with some wonderful friends of mom's and mine who came and chased me away for awhile. They helped me cope with my pain and sadness. My brother Jim came from Edmonton and we went to Banff for a day. That too was respite care I needed and I came back refreshed. Mother had such a strong heart and healthy body that her dying was prolonged. After I had been with her for almost a month, her doctor suggested that I should consider going back to work. That was a tough decision and one I couldn't make in a hurry. I discussed it with two very dear, longtime friends and they agreed with the doctor, but no one pushed me. They said they would visit mom daily. Finally, with much thought and prayer, I made the decision to return to Springfield. When the morning to leave arrived, I was ambivalent and, as I write this, again feel the pain. Could I really go and leave my mom, knowing I may never see her again? I'm not sure if I'd have been strong enough to do it alone, even knowing God was with me. But my dear nephew Bob was there to comfort me and to drive me to the airport. Together we went to see mom, gave her a hug and a kiss, said good-bye and quickly left the room without looking back.

I was only back 10 days when I received a telephone call from my friend Lillian: "Your mother went upstairs this morning." At first I didn't understand what she was telling me, so finally she said, "Your mother died this morning." And so back to Calgary I went as quickly as the plane could fly. When I arrived, my younger brother Jim and his wife had already taken care of the immediate tasks to be done following a death. It did not fill any need of mine to see mom again — I had said my good-byes just 10 days before and her wishes were to be cremated. On reflection, I have no feeling of guilt about not being present when she died. I had given her all I could while she lived. I also knew she was well-loved and cared for until the end by Pastor Del, my dear friends and a loving God. We had a beautiful memorial service for her in the garden at Bethany. She loved music, and so the organ was playing some of her favorite hymns while many of her Bethany friends and old family friends gathered to say a final farewell to Hannah Marie.

I don't recall doing much grieving until I went to China with a group of SIU faculty three months later. It was another dream come true, and yet I remember very little of what I saw or did. I do remember feeling very sad and crying when we were in Shanghai on October 5th — mother's 90th birthday. I also vividly recall a feeling of excitement when I realized our next stop was to be Guangzhou (formerly called Canton). Here I had made plans, before leaving Springfield, for my beloved "Amah" — Ah Yoke — to meet me. She lived in a village about 50 miles outside Guangzhou. She had loved and cared for me in a very special way during my seven years in Singapore and Malaya. Saying good-bye to her when I came home in 1967 had been like losing a loved one through death, since I really didn't believe we would ever see each other again. But there I was, grieving the death of my own mother and at the same time joyfully hoping to see Ah Yoke again, who was also very much a mother figure to me.

The day after we arrived in Guangzhou, there she was with her nephew, his wife and two children. Words wouldn't come at first. We just stood and cried and hugged each other. What a reunion! To hear her call me "Missy" again — the word still rings in my ears. There wasn't much sleep for either of us that night, because our group had to leave for home the next morning. Ah Yoke would not leave until she had me safely on the bus. Ah Yoke could neither read or write but could speak four languages. And she was blessed with a big heart and a brilliant mind. When I returned to Springfield, we were able to continue our communication with the help of a Chinese translator.

Four years later, in 1988, a miracle happened. Terry Mast, a co-author of this book and SIU faculty member, led a small group from SIU to visit its sister medical school, Sun Yat Sen University of Medical Sciences, in Guangzhou. He knew about Ah Yoke and, with help from the Sun Yat Sen staff, arrangements were made for him to visit her village. You can imagine my joy when he returned with pictures of himself with Ah Yoke. Their meeting was especially significant, because Ah Yoke died two years later. But she, like my mom, will live in my heart forever.

Mother's death changed my planning for holidays and special occasions, especially Christmas. From the time my dad died in 1968 until her death, we had enjoyed vacation times together and every Christmas but one. She was dearly loved by many, had a great zest for life and was always thoughtful of others. Much as I missed her, I suddenly realized I was free to make other choices regarding my work and leisure time.

The word retirement became a reality for the first time in my life. Although I had many interests and hobbies, my career as a nurse had always taken priority. I had been blessed with opportunities that provided me with unusual experiences and brought many new challenges. I believe some of the gifts God gave me were courage and faith to face the unknown, and a healthy mind and body to do the work I was called to do. Now facing me were the many big questions associated with retirement.

Loss and change evoke some of the same feelings associated with dying and death. My life's work had provided me with some of the tools I needed, but no change had seemed as

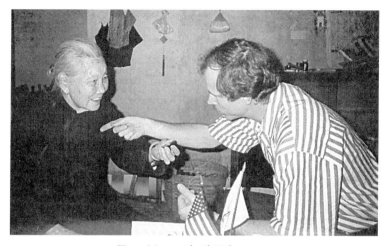

Terry Mast with Ah Yoke, 1988.

final as this one. I experienced considerable ambivalence: part of me wanted the freedom of retirement, while the other part wanted to continue teaching. I did have tenure until I was 70, so there was no immediate hurry. When I finally made my decision, it felt like a weight had been lifted off my shoulders. I gave myself a year: time for some anticipatory grief and tending to unfinished business. The one major issue I didn't deal with until about two months before my retirement date was where I was going to live. In my mind I assumed I'd return to Canada. But my Springfield friends assumed I'd continue to make my home in Springfield. The love and care that poured forth from my extended family and church friends made me feel very wanted. I heard such comments as, "It's O.K. to retire, but why do you have to leave us?" After much thought and feeling, I opted to stay in Springfield, but with one proviso — I would retain my Canadian citizenship.

Although I was responsible for making the final decision, I didn't have to do it alone. And I have no regrets.

As I reflect back on my life from the time I moved to Springfield until my retirement in July 1985, I'm grateful for the many blessings I received. The people I met, taught with, laughed and cried with and walked the last journey with taught me much more than can be contained in this book. Because I believe in becoming involved professionally if I wish to be a helper/caregiver, I have needed to learn ways to become detached for my own survival. But even those attachments described in the chapters of this book are at a different level emotionally than with family and close friends when crisis or death occurs. By now I know myself fairly well and I have the capacity to dig fairly deep roots wherever I live. Some caring, special friendships have grown as a result. I cherish and nurture them and know that, even when physically apart, we are together emotionally and spiritually.

When serious illness or death has occurred to people very dear to me, being involved has been very painful. Tragedy suddenly struck one of my extended families when one of their teenage sons, Paul, was killed suddenly in a head-on car accident. His friend riding with him was also killed. I received a phone call early in the morning from Jay's family. It was amazing how quickly our own support group gathered and things happened, even though we all moved like robots. Emotions ran rampant at times, with silence, tears and hugging intermingled. The two days before the funeral and interment were long and sad. The two boys were buried side by side, with many of their classmates, families and friends huddled closely on the hillside for the final farewell. It was a tragedy with no answer to the question, "Why?"

Paul's sudden death threw his family, extended family, schoolmates and friends into facing the ramifications of immediate grief. There was no time for the preparation that anticipatory grief can give. We each had our own grieving to do, but more important was trying to support his immediate family. I believe we were sensitive to their needs for privacy and time to do their own grief work. We will never know the deep pain they suffered, but they did not run away. They are a deeply Christian family and as they began to heal, Paul's mother told me how her faith sustained her. Viktor Frankl in his book *Man's Search for Meaning* says, "If there is a purpose in life at all, there must be a purpose in suffering and dying. But no man can tell another what this purpose is. Each must find out for himself."

Several Canadian friends with whom I had a close relationship have died in the last few years with terminal illnesses. I have not been able to be present with them in their dying as I was with my friend Jack, whose story was told earlier in this book. Lily had a long battle with cancer of the intestines. She received massive doses of chemotherapy with many side effects, including loss of her hair. She also had to learn to live with a colostomy. I visited her several times in Saskatoon and each time she would say, "When are you coming home?" One of my friends, living near Lily, took her a rose from me frequently. I had planned to visit her just a few days before Christmas. She knew I was coming, but she died before I got there. One of the nurses who was with her in her dying later told me her last spoken words were, "Norma's coming December 20th." It was difficult to let her go from this distance, even though my head told me Lily was now at peace. I still miss the beautiful letters she wrote me, our phone calls, her love for living and reaching out to others even during her own pain and suffering. But our love for each other will always remain.

The deaths of Lily and a few other special friends who died in Canada who I could not be with have forced me to face the issue of being far away and unable to say "Good-bye." I found myself feeling very sad, helpless and isolated. Again, I have found my tears a gift and learned the importance of spending time with Norma. I have also learned to reach out for help to friends I trust who listen to my stories, give me hugs, cry with me and pray with me. I am truly blessed. Friday morning breakfasts with Terry and Jay are one of the highlights of my week. Thank you, my fellow travellers, for this special time of telling our stories — listening, sharing and caring.

In April 1991, I was again fortunate enough to be off to China, this time going alone, but with a special mission to teach for three weeks. I had been invited as a visiting professor to SIU's sister school in Guangzhou. My assignment was to teach medical and nursing students and graduates some of the psycho-social needs of patients and families, with particular emphasis on the terminally ill and aging. What a challenge! Most of the students spoke only limited English, so an interpreter was essential, and they gave me the best. Her name was Hui Qing. She had graduated from the prestigious Peking Union Medical College in the 1930s with a baccalaureate degree in nursing — a rarity then and equally so today. Having once been a dean at one of the nursing schools in China, she is still one of the leaders in nursing in China. How privileged I was to have her as my interpreter, guide, friend and advocate. Without her it would have been impossible for me to teach four to six hours some days, all through an interpreter. We were the model of teamwork. I also had many opportunities to visit at the bedside, both in the countryside and in the large teaching hospitals. There was no way to measure the effects of my teaching. I gave them all I could — me. Kahlil Gibran said, "You give but little when you give of your possessions. It is when you give of yourself that you truly give." And they gave me so much love in return. My long-time love and admiration for the Chinese only deepened. I have been richly blessed.

I continue to thrive with retirement and the many doors that still open. I trust that my thirst for new knowledge and adventures will continue as exciting happenings move us into tomorrow and the new century.

This book is especially written for educators of medical students, nursing students, seminary students or others who want to learn the skills required to walk the journey with dying patients and their families. We have attempted to write a brief description of some of the essential components used as a caregiver walking bedside these courageous people. A bibliography has also been carefully selected — each book addressing one or more of the specifiic subject matters.

1. **Communication: The common denominator**
    John Powell in his book *Will the Real Me Please Stand Up?* says "Human communication is the lifeblood and heartbeat of every relationship." Many of us have difficulty in communicating at the level necessary to assist the patient and family in their living and their dying. But we all can learn ways to improve our communication skills if we choose.
    How well do you communicate with your fellow human beings? How could you improve your communication?

2. **Who Am I?**
    I believe the beginning of my journey was discovering who I really am. For many of us this may be a new journey towards becoming a fully functioning human being. We know, as human beings, we have two major parts of self — our external and our internal self. Our external self is our physical structure which tells the outside world who we are. Much of the health care system is based on the breakdown of the physical body and the attempts made to cure it — to fix the external self that is disease oriented. Often the treatment plan leaves out **care**. As Randy's chemotherapy failed to **cure** his leukemia it was more important than ever that his phy-

sician, nurses and others **care** for him. To become a fully functioning caregiver it is essential that we develop the other part
of selves — our internal selves. Dag Hammerskold wrote:
"The longest journey of any person is the journey inward."

3. Gifts

For many this discovery of your internal self may be a new
experience. Personally I found it frightening but also very
exciting. When I discovered that perhaps the greatest gift I
had to give in a relationship was myself, I truly understood
the meaning of the words care and love. And to accept my
tears as a gift to give, not only freed me from the embarrass-
ment equated with tears but allowed me to claim them as my
gift to give away. Each of us needs to affirm our own unique
gifts before we can give them away.

What are your gifts?

4. Truth-Telling — Hope

Dying patients deprived of truth, are deprived of opportunities for healing. The patient's physician is the member of
the team responsible for telling the truth and yet seldom does
medical education provide guidelines for this universal
process. Nurses, social workers, pastors and others who care
for patients need to recognize the need for truth-telling also.
Hospice teaches that people do better with the truth.

Many physicians and the public itself still fear that in
telling the dying patient the truth you may take hope away.
Norman Cousin's book *Head First: The Biology of Hope*
addresses this topic and is an excellent source for all of us. He
says, "People tell me not to offer hope unless I know hope to
be real. I don't know enough to say that hope can't be real.
Illness is a terrifying experience. Something is happening that

people don't know how to deal with. They are reaching out not just for medical help but for ways of thinking about catastrophic illness. They are reaching out for hope. No matter how small the chance of recovery may be, reassurance is a lifeline that connects the physician and patient in a joint venture."

If Gary and Marilyn had not recognized the importance of truth-telling in their own relationship I am certain Gary would not have had the courage to tell his children, wife and mother that he was dying and ask them to pray for him. Without this open communication I wonder if this family would have been able to have the quality time together they did in the midst of Gary's dying.

Are you comfortable with truth-telling, and with helping families be truthful with each other? Is there then one version of the truth? Do different people have different truths?

5. Caring

I find Henri Nowen's description of **care** very helpful. In his book *Out of Solitude* he says that the word care comes from the Gothic word kara. It means to grieve, to experience sorrow, to enter into the pain with someone. He says "Every human being has a great, yet often unknown, gift to care, to be compassionate, to become present to the other, to listen, to hear, to receive." This requires each of us to examine our own **listening** skills. They can be learned but they are more than mechanical techniques. Most of us, when we should be in the listener's role, feel compelled to be speakers. To enter into a truly caring role requires me to listen with my heart as well as my senses. The really good listener listens for the 'context' of the sharing as well as the 'content'. This demands feeling comfortable in silence and being able to literally reach out and touch someone with a tender and loving hand.

How good a listener are you? Do you feel comfortable with silence? Are you able to touch and hug your fellow human being?

6. Pain — Physical, Emotional, Spiritual

Pain may be considered in three parts — all intertwining and affecting each other. It is important for us to have a basic understanding of each if we are going to give total patient care.

a. *Physical Pain*

One of the cornerstones on which hospice was founded was pain and symptom control. Teaching the patient to manage his/her own pain, through administering their own medication, has been a major breakthrough. But physicians and nurses have also been challenged to learn much more about painkillers and their administration. I have witnessed this dramatic change over the past 20 years — I have watched a person move from writhing pain to almost absence of pain and see them smile again, live again. Gary was enabled to live, during his last few weeks of life, because of effective pain control carefully monitored by his loving wife.

b. *Emotional Pain — Feelings*

Many doctors and nurses fail to appreciate fully that pain is not simply a physical sensation. Many emotional factors lower the pain threshold, such as anxiety, fear, anger, sadness, depression — our feelings. Much of our society encourages people to deny their feelings, to put up a good front, to "keep a stiff upper lip." The caregiver cannot help the patient and family without learning the therapeutic use of his or her own inner feelings. In Williams' book *Grief Ministry* she says, "Feelings must be named and acknowledged in order to experience inner freedom and clarity." She encourages each of us to first become aware of our own inner feelings. Only then are we able to help the patients express some of their own feelings: *how long will I have to live, doctor; why do I have to suffer?*

c. *Spiritual Pain — Suffering*

Some of the feelings just described with emotional pain are present also with spiritual pain. Our own faith and religion sometimes influence our meaning of suffering. Many today still believe that disease is punishment for wrong-doing. Not only does the patient suffer but also the family and caregivers.

We need to search alone and together for some meaning. The suffering we have in common can be the occasion for a healing relationship of love and acceptance.

One way to enhance this relationship is through prayer. It is communication with God — however or whatever one believes God to be. Williams says, "By your prayerful and loving presence to persons who are on a journey of illness, loss, aging, death or other human pain, you are like Raphael, the angel. Your faithful companionship assures people that all will be well and that the road is safe."

Nan told me how much better she slept on the nights she had phoned me and asked me to pray for her. George, also, said he found help and peace when his minister visited him and had prayer. When I was with George and Marjorie in the evening we had prayer together before I left. Prayer is another way to reach out and help each other — the patient, the family and the caregiver.

I believe that Ann's deep spiritual belief enabled her to walk the long journey with her mother. She said, "The Lord and I spend a lot of time together. We deal with our issues and the spirit and I are pretty much in touch on that."

7. Conferences

There are two specific conferences referenced in this book that were essential in planning for the care of the individual patient and family.

a. *Patient Care Conference*

Although such a conference is seldom organized I believe Esther's story would have been very different without it. She had made a very major request — to pull the plug as she was ready to die. This issue was rarely discussed or considered in the late 1970s. The physician was the key player in this drama. He was willing to grant Esther her wish but knew he could not do it alone. My role as a consultant in Esther's story was important. My education and clinical experience, both in working with dying patients and in planning patient care conferences, provided me with the qualifications needed for this arduous task.

b. *A Family Conference*

The family (which includes the patient) is the unit of care. In order for the whole family to receive quality care during the living, dying process it is important that all members have knowledge of the diagnosis, causes of disease and the psycho-social aspects which accompany this. This requires effective communication — truth-telling. But it is often hedged around with difficulties such as fear, anxiety, anger. Open communication evokes feelings in the patient, the family and the caregivers themselves. Game playing often occurs — 'Who knows what', 'Don't tell her — she can't take it' are remarks often heard.

This lack of open awareness of all the family is quite evident in Randy's story when he went home for Christmas. Hearing his story when he returned prompted me to discuss with the head nurse and Randy's physician the need for a family conference. You have read the positive results. This shows how family counseling can allow the family to grow together at the same time and make the best use of each day — living, loving and caring.

The issues surrounding the family conference in Nan's story are different but I believe it began some forgiveness, mending of fences, and saying good-byes, that Nan could help the family with before she died.

8. Grief

There are two kinds of grief we experience, except in the situation of sudden death. The first kind is anticipatory or preparatory grief. It can be experienced both by the dying person and by those close to the patient. It has much of the same dynamics as grief after death. George's story illustrates for us how much living and loving he and Marjorie did while he was dying. She told me she believes she did much of her grieving while he was alive and able to help her. He also gave her a gift when he gave her his blessing to marry again.

The family conference with George's four daughters was also an important piece of anticipatory grief and a coming together of the family unit.

Ann's story shows the aftermath of sudden death and the lack of an opportunity to say good-bye to a loved one. The grieving process is often delayed for a long time. In her husband Pete's situation, it was for 14 years. But his feelings were finally released while Ann was grieving the anticipated death of her mother. He described this as having a heavy brick lifted from his shoulders. Also his ability to finally begin his own grieving enabled him to help Ann and her family, later the same day, be present with Floy in her dying and to say a final farewell to their mother.

Grief work cannot be done alone — it is truly a team effort. We need to remember we all have many gifts.

What are your gifts? How can you help in the grieving process?

9. Celebration

Norman Cousins, a humanitarian, teacher, communicator and writer has had a considerable influence concerning my learning, thinking and practicing in the field of nursing and medicine. One of his greatest attributes that I admire is a positive attitude. His research showed the rapidly mounting scientific evidence that hope, faith, love, will to live, purpose, laughter and festivity can enhance the environment of medical treatment and/or help to combat serious disease. In my book this calls for celebration — at the end of the journey. Some of the families in our book have shared with us their celebration — for the life lived of their loved one, now dead. I call this a marriage of joy and sadness. In Jack's story, Benny Goodman's music was piped into his memorial service and later we celebrated his life at the faculty club.

Learn what you can from the families you met in this book — (each of us has our own opinions about how best to help the patient and family cope with dying and death). The stories told in this book are my stories and how I helped to the best of my ability. May they be a guide for you.

Norma Wylie

REFERENCES

Cousins, Norman. *Anatomy of an Illness.* New York: Bantam, 1981.

Cousins, Norman. *Head First: The Biology of Hope.* New York: E.P. Dutton, 1989.

Davidson, Glen W. *The Hospice: Development and Administration.* Washington, D.C.: Hemisphere, 1978.

Frankl, Viktor E. *Man's Search for Meaning,* New York: Washington Square Press, 1985.

Kübler-Ross, Elisabeth. *On Death and Dying.* London: MacMillan, 1969.

Kushner, Harold S. *When Bad Things Happen to Good People.* New York: Schochen Books, 1981.

Lewis, C.S. *A Grief Observed.* New York: Bantam Books, 1980.

Mace, Nancy L., and Peter V. Rabins. *The 36-Hour Day.* Baltimore: John Hopkins University Press, 1981.

MacFarland, John Robert. *Now That I Have Cancer I Am Whole.* Kansas City: Andrews and McMeel Universal Press, 1993.

Nowen, Henri J. M. *Out of Solitude.* Notre Dame, Indiana: Ave Maria Press, 1974.

Pope, Robert. *Illness and Healing: Images of Cancer.* Hantsport, Nova Scotia: Lancelot Press, 1991.

Saunders, Cecily. *The Management of Terminal Disease.* London: Edward Arnold, 1978.

Saunders, Cecily, Mary Baines and Robert Dunlop. *Living with Dying: A Guide to Palliative Care.* New York: Oxford University Press, 1995.

Williams, Donna Reilly and Sturzl, Jo Ann. *Grief Ministry.* San Jose, California: Resource Publications, Inc., 1992.

Wylie, Norma. *The Role of the Nurse in Clinical Medical Education.* Springfield, Ill.: Southern Illinois University School of Medicine, 1988.